3A

FOUR CORNERS

Second Edition

Student's Book
with Digital Pack

JACK C. RICHARDS & DAVID BOHLKE

Shaftesbury Road, Cambridge CB2 8EA, United Kingdom

One Liberty Plaza, 20th Floor, New York, NY 10006, USA

477 Williamstown Road, Port Melbourne, VIC 3207, Australia

314–321, 3rd Floor, Plot 3, Splendor Forum, Jasola District Centre, New Delhi – 110025, India

103 Penang Road, #05–06/07, Visioncrest Commercial, Singapore 238467

Cambridge University Press & Assessment is a department of the University of Cambridge.

We share the University's mission to contribute to society through the pursuit of education, learning and research at the highest international levels of excellence.

www.cambridge.org
Information on this title: www.cambridge.org/9781009286541

© Cambridge University Press & Assessment 2012, 2019, 2023

First published 2012
Second edition 2019

20 19 18 17 16 15 14 13 12 11 10 9 8 7 6 5 4

Printed in Malaysia by Vivar Printing

A catalogue record for this publication is available from the British Library

ISBN 978-1-009-28653-4   Student's Book with Digital Pack 3
ISBN 978-1-009-28654-1   Student's Book with Digital Pack 3A
ISBN 978-1-009-28655-8   Student's Book with Digital Pack 3B
ISBN 978-1-108-55995-9   Teacher's Edition with Complete Assessment Program 3
ISBN 978-1-009-28650-3   Full Contact with Digital Pack 3
ISBN 978-1-009-28651-0   Full Contact with Digital Pack 3A
ISBN 978-1-009-28652-7   Full Contact with Digital Pack 3B
ISBN 978-1-009-28595-7   Presentation Plus Level 3

Additional resources for this publication at www.cambridge.org/fourcorners

Cambridge University Press & Assessment has no responsibility for the persistence or accuracy of URLs for external or third-party internet websites referred to in this publication and does not guarantee that any content on such websites is, or will remain, accurate or appropriate.

Authors' acknowledgments

Many people contributed to the development of *Four Corners*. The authors and publisher would like to particularly thank the following **reviewers**:

Nele Noe, **Academy for Educational Development, Qatar Independent Secondary School for Girls**, Doha, Qatar; Pablo Stucchi, **Antonio Raimondi School** and **Instituto San Ignacio de Loyola**, Lima, Peru; Nadeen Katz, **Asia University**, Tokyo, Japan; Tim Vandenhoek, **Asia University**, Tokyo, Japan; Celso Frade and Sonia Maria Baccari de Godoy, **Associação Alumni**, São Paulo, Brazil; Rosane Bandeira, **Atlanta Idiomas**, Manaus, Brazil; Cacilda Reis da Silva, **Atlanta Idiomas**, Manaus, Brazil; Gretta Sicsu, **Atlanta Idiomas**, Manaus, Brazil; Naila Maria Cañiso Ferreira, **Atlanta Idiomas**, Manaus, Brazil; Hothnã Moraes de Souza Neto, **Atlanta Idiomas**, Manaus, Brazil; Jacqueline Kurtzious, **Atlanta Idiomas**, Manaus, Brazil; José Menezes Ribeiro Neto, **Atlanta Idiomas**, Manaus, Brazil; Sheila Ribeiro Cordeiro, **Atlanta Idiomas**, Manaus, Brazil; Juliana Fernandes, **Atlanta Idiomas**, Manaus, Brazil; Aline Alexandrina da Silva, **Atlanta Idiomas**, Manaus, Brazil; Kari Miller, **Binational Center**, Quito, Ecuador; Alex K. Oliveira, **Boston University**, Boston, MA, USA; Noriko Furuya, **Bunka Gakuen University**, Tokyo, Japan; Robert Hickling, **Bunka Gakuen University**, Tokyo, Japan; John D. Owen, **Bunka Gakuen University**, Tokyo, Japan; Elisabeth Blom, **Casa Thomas Jefferson**, Brasília, Brazil; Lucilena Oliveira Andrade, **Centro Cultural Brasil Estados Unidos (CCBEU Belém)**, Belém, Brazil; Marcelo Franco Borges, **Centro Cultural Brasil Estados Unidos (CCBEU Belém)**, Belém, Brazil; Geysa de Azevedo Moreira, **Centro Cultural Brasil Estados Unidos (CCBEU Belém)**, Belém, Brazil; Anderson Felipe Barbosa Negrão, **Centro Cultural Brasil Estados Unidos (CCBEU Belém)**, Belém, Brazil; Henry Grant, **CCBEU – Campinas**, Campinas, Brazil; Maria do Rosário, **CCBEU – Franca**, Franca, Brazil; Ane Cibele Palma, **CCBEU Inter Americano**, Curitiba, Brazil; Elen Flavia Penques da Costa, **Centro de Cultura Idiomas – Taubaté**, Taubaté, Brazil; Inara Lúcia Castillo Couto, **CEL LEP – São Paulo**, São Paulo, Brazil; Sonia Patricia Cardoso, **Centro de Idiomas Universidad Manuela Beltrán**, Barrio Cedritos, Colombia; Geraldine Itiago Losada, **Centro Universitario Grupo Sol (Musali)**, Mexico City, Mexico; Nick Hilmers, **DePaul University**, Chicago, IL, USA; Monica L. Montemayor Menchaca, **EDIMSA**, Metepec, Mexico; Angela Whitby, **Edu-Idiomas Language School**, Cholula, Puebla, Mexico; Mary Segovia, **El Monte Rosemead Adult School**, Rosemead, CA, USA; Dr. Deborah Aldred, **ELS Language Centers, Middle East Region**, Abu Dhabi, United Arab Emirates; Leslie Lott, **Embassy CES**, Ft. Lauderdale, FL, USA; M. Martha Lengeling, **Escuela de Idiomas**, Guanajuato, Mexico; Pablo Frias, **Escuela de Idiomas UNAPEC**, Santo Domingo, Dominican Republic; Tracy Vanderhoek, **ESL Language Center**, Toronto, Canada; Kris Vicca and Michael McCollister, **Feng Chia University**, Taichung, Taiwan; Flávia Patricia do Nascimento Martins, **First Idiomas**, Sorocaba, Brazil; Andrea Taylor, **Florida State University in Panama**, Panamá, Panama; Carlos Lizárraga González, **Grupo Educativo Angloamericano**, Mexico City, Mexico; Bo-Kyung Lee, **Hankuk University of Foreign Studies**, Seoul, South Korea; Dr. Martin Endley, **Hanyang University**, Seoul, South Korea; Mauro Luiz Pinheiro, **IBEU Ceará**, Ceará, Brazil; Ana Lúcia da Costa Maia de Almeida, **IBEU Copacabana**, Copacabana, Brazil; Maristela Silva, **ICBEU Manaus**, Manaus, Brazil; Magaly Mendes Lemos, **ICBEU São José dos Campos**, São José dos Campos, Brazil; Augusto Pelligrini Filho, **ICBEU São Luis**, São Luis, Brazil; Leonardo Mercado, **ICPNA**, Lima, Peru; Lucia Rangel Lugo, **Instituto Tecnológico de San Luis Potosí**, San Luis Potosí, Mexico; Maria Guadalupe Hernández Lozada, **Instituto Tecnológico de Tlalnepantla**, Tlalnepantla de Baz, Mexico; Karen Stewart, **International House Veracruz**, Veracruz, Mexico; Tom David, **Japan College of Foreign Languages**, Tokyo, Japan; Andy Burki, **Korea University, International Foreign Language School**, Seoul, South Korea; Jinseo Noh, **Kwangwoon University**, Seoul, South Korea; Neil Donachey, **La Salle Junior and Senior High School**, Kagoshima, Japan; Rich Hollingworth, **La Salle Junior and Senior High School**, Kagoshima, Japan; Quentin Kum, **La Salle Junior and Senior High School**, Kagoshima, Japan; Geoff Oliver, **La Salle Junior and Senior High School**, Kagoshima, Japan; Martin Williams, **La Salle Junior and Senior High School**, Kagoshima, Japan; Nadezhda Nazarenko, **Lone Star College**, Houston, TX, USA; Carolyn Ho, **Lone Star College-Cy-Fair**, Cypress, TX, USA; Kaoru Kuwajima, **Meijo University**, Nogoya, Japan; Alice Ya-fen Chou, **National Taiwan University of Science and Technology**, Taipei, Taiwan; Raymond Dreyer, **Northern Essex Community College**, Lawrence, MA, USA; Mary Keter Terzian Megale, **One Way Línguas-Suzano**, São Paulo, Brazil; B. Greg Dunne, **Osaka Shoin Women's University**, Higashi-Osaka, Japan; Robert Maran, **Osaka Shoin Women's University**, Higashi-Osaka, Japan; Bonnie Cheeseman, **Pasadena Community College** and **UCLA American Language Center**, Los Angeles, CA, USA; Simon Banha, **Phil Young's English School**, Curitiba, Brazil; Oh Jun Il, **Pukyong National University**, Busan, South Korea; Carmen Gehrke, **Quatrum English Schools**, Porto Alegre, Brazil; John Duplice, **Rikkyo University**, Tokyo, Japan; Mengjiao Wu, **Shanghai Maritime University**, Shanghai, China; Wilzania da Silva Nascimento, **Senac**, Manaus, Brazil; Miva Silva Kingston, **Senac**, Manaus, Brazil; Lais Lima, **Senac**, Manaus, Brazil; Yuan-hsun Chuang, **Soo Chow University**, Taipei, Taiwan; Wen hsiang Su, **Shih Chien University Kaohsiung Campus**, Kaohsiung, Taiwan; Lynne Kim, **Sun Moon University (Institute for Language Education)**, Cheon An City, Chung Nam, South Korea; Regina Ramalho, **Talken English School**, Curitiba, Brazil; Tatiana Mendonça, **Talken English School**, Curitiba, Brazil; Ricardo Todeschini, **Talken English School**, Curitiba, Brazil; Monica Carvalho da Rocha, **Talken English School**, Joinville, Brazil; Karina Schoene, **Talken English School**, Joinville, Brazil; Diãna Peña Munoz and Zira Kuri, **The Anglo**, Mexico City, Mexico; Christopher Modell, **Tokai University**, Tokyo, Japan; Song-won Kim, **TTI (Teacher's Training Institute)**, Seoul, South Korea; Nancy Alarcón, **UNAM FES Zaragoza Language Center**, Mexico City, Mexico; Laura Emilia Fierro López, **Universidad Autónoma de Baja California**, Mexicali, Mexico; María del Rocío Domínguez Gaona, **Universidad Autónoma de Baja California**, Tijuana, Mexico; Saul Santos Garcia, **Universidad Autónoma de Nayarit**, Nayarit, Mexico; Christian Meléndez, **Universidad Católica de El Salvador**, San Salvador, El Salvador; Irasema Mora Pablo, **Universidad de Guanajuato**, Guanajuato, Mexico; Alberto Peto, **Universidad de Oaxaca**, Tehuantepec, Mexico; Carolina Rodriguez Beltan, **Universidad Manuela Beltrán, Centro Colombo Americano**, and **Universidad Jorge Tadeo Lozano**, Bogotá, Colombia; Nidia Milena Molina Rodriguez, **Universidad Manuela Beltrán** and **Universidad Militar Nueva Granada**, Bogotá, Colombia; Yolima Perez Arias, **Universidad Nacional de Colombia**, Bogotá, Colombia; Héctor Vázquez García, **Universidad Nacional Autónoma de Mexico**, Mexico City, Mexico; Pilar Barrera, **Universidad Técnica de Ambato**, Ambato, Ecuador; Doborah Hulston, **University of Regina**, Regina, Canada; Rebecca J. Shelton, **Valparaiso University, Interlink Language Center**, Valparaiso, IN, USA; Tae Lee, **Yonsei University**, Seodaemun-gu, Seoul, South Korea; Claudia Thereza Nascimento Mendes, **York Language Institute**, Rio de Janeiro, Brazil; Jamila Jenny Hakam, **ELT Consultant**, Muscat, Oman; Stephanie Smith, **ELT Consultant**, Austin, TX, USA.

Scope and sequence

LEVEL 3	Learning outcomes	Grammar	Vocabulary
Classroom language Page 2			
Unit 1 Pages 3–12			
Education A *I'm taking six classes* B *You're not allowed to…* C *My behavior* D *Education controversy*	**Students can…** ☑ ask and talk about routines ☑ express prohibition and obligation ☑ ask and talk about feelings and reactions ☑ discuss advantages and disadvantages	Simple present vs. present continuous Zero conditional	School subjects Feelings and emotions
Unit 2 Pages 13–22			

Personal stories
A *What were you doing?*
B *Guess what!*
 	
C *I was really frightened!*
D *How embarrassing!*
	Students can…
	☑ describe what was happening in the past
	☑ announce news
	☑ close a conversation
	☑ tell personal stories
	☑ describe embarrassing moments
		Past continuous vs.
		  simple past
		Participial adjectives
			Sentence adverbs
			Verbs to describe
			  reactions

Unit 3 Pages 23–32			
Style and fashion A *Fashion trends* B *Does this come in…?* C *The latest look* D *Views on fashion*	**Students can…** ☑ ask about and describe past fashions ☑ ask where something is in a store ☑ ask for a specific product ☑ express opinions about style and fashion ☑ ask and talk about current fashions	*Used to* Defining relative clauses	Fashion statements Clothing styles
Unit 4 Pages 33–42			
Interesting lives A *Have you ever been on TV?* B *What I mean is…* C *Life experiences* D *What a life!*	**Students can…** ☑ ask and talk about life experiences ☑ check and clarify meaning ☑ describe details of their experiences ☑ ask and talk about a memorable experience	Present perfect Present perfect vs. simple past	Experiences Fun things to do
Unit 5 Pages 43–52			
Our world A *Older, taller, and more famous* B *I don't believe it!* C *World geography* D *Natural wonders*	**Students can…** ☑ Compare human-made structures ☑ express disbelief ☑ say that they don't know something ☑ ask and talk about geographical features ☑ describe natural wonders in their country	Comparatives *Not as…as* Superlatives	Human-made wonders Geographical features
Unit 6 Pages 53–62			

Organizing your time
A *A busy week*
B *Can I take a message?*
 	
C *Can you do me a favor?*
D *Perspectives on time*
	Students can…
	☑ ask and talk about weekend plans
	☑ offer to take a message
	☑ leave a message
	☑ make requests, promises, and offers
	☑ discuss ways to manage time effectively
		Present tenses used for
		  future
		Requests
		Promises and offers with
		  will
			Commitments
			Favors

Functional language	Listening and Pronunciation	Reading and Writing	Speaking
Interactions: Expressing prohibition Expressing obligation	**Listening:** Office rules An interview about homeschooling **Pronunciation:** Stress and rhythm	**Reading:** "Are Video Games Educational?" An article **Writing:** Advantages and disadvantages of distance education	• Information exchange about school and work • *Keep talking*: "Find someone who" activity about everyday activities • List of class rules • Information exchange about personal behavior • *Keep talking*: Comparison of behaviors • Discussion about distance education
Interactions: Announcing news Closing a conversation	**Listening:** News about other people A camping trip **Pronunciation:** Intonation in complex sentences	**Reading:** "Embarrassing Experiences" An article **Writing:** An embarrassing moment	• Group story about a past event • *Keep talking*: Description of simultaneous past actions • Celebrity news • Personal stories and anecdotes • *Keep talking*: Picture stories • Descriptions of embarrassing moments
Interactions: Asking where things are Asking for an alternative	**Listening:** Clothing purchases An interview with a fashion designer **Pronunciation:** *Used to* and *use to*	**Reading:** "Dress to Impress" An article **Writing:** Class survey	• Interview about style and fashion • *Keep talking*: Comparison of two people's past and present styles • Role play of a shopping situation • Opinions on fashion and style • *Keep talking*: Interview about what's hot • Class survey about style and fashion
Interactions: Checking meaning Clarifying meaning	**Listening:** Unusual habits An interview with a grandmother **Pronunciation:** Contrastive stress in responses	**Reading:** "The Life of an Astronaut" An interview **Writing:** Interesting people, places, or things	• Interview about experiences • *Keep talking*: Information exchange about experiences never had • Information exchange about unusual habits • True and false information about life experiences • *Keep talking*: "Find someone who" activity about everyday experiences • Description of an interesting person or place
Interactions: Expressing disbelief Saying you don't know	**Listening:** An interesting city The Great Barrier Reef **Pronunciation:** Intonation in tag questions	**Reading:** "Seven Wonders of the Natural World" An article **Writing:** A natural wonder	• Comparison of different places • *Keep talking*: Information gap activity about impressive places • Information exchange about human-made structures • Discussion about experiences in different places • *Keep talking*: Advice for foreign visitors • List of the most wonderful places in the country
Interactions: Offering to take a message Leaving a message	**Listening:** Weekend plans Phone messages **Pronunciation:** Reduction of *could you* and *would you*	**Reading:** "Time and Culture" An article **Writing:** Tips for success	• "Find someone who" activity about weekend plans • *Keep talking*: Information exchange about upcoming plans • Role play with phone messages • Class favors, offers, and promises • *Keep talking*: Role play with requests • Quiz about overdoing things

Classroom language

A 🎧 Complete the conversations with the correct sentences. Then listen and check your answers.

What page are we on?   ✓ Excuse me. I'm very sorry I'm late.
Can you repeat that, please?   May I go to the restroom, please?
What's our homework?   Which role do you want to play?

A <u>Excuse me. I'm sorry I'm late.</u>

B That's OK. Next time try to arrive on time.

A _____

B Thirteen. We're doing the Warm-up for Unit 2.

A _____

B Yes. I said, "Please work with a partner."

A _____

B I'll be Student A. You can be Student B.

A _____

B No problem. Please try to be quick.

A _____

B Please complete the activities for Unit 2 in your workbook.

B PAIR WORK Practice the conversations.

1 Education

Lesson A
- School subjects
- Simple present vs. present continuous

Lesson B
- Expressing prohibition
- Expressing obligation

Lesson C
- Feelings and emotions
- Zero conditional

Lesson D
- Reading "Are Video Games Educational?"
- Writing: Distance education

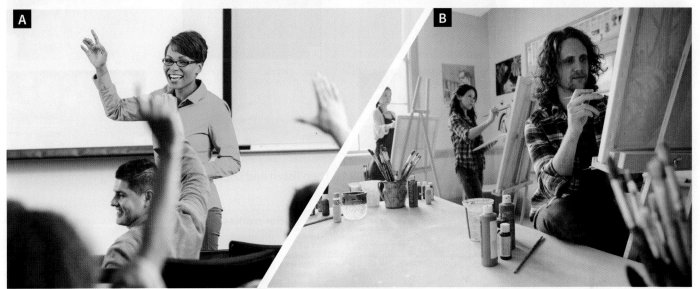

Warm Up

A Describe the pictures. What do you see? What are the students doing?

B How are the classrooms similar or different from your own classroom experiences?

A I'm taking six classes.

1 Vocabulary School subjects

A 🎧 Match the words and the pictures. Then listen and check your answers.

- a algebra
- b art
- c biology
- d chemistry
- e geometry
- f history
- g music
- ✓ h physics
- i world geography

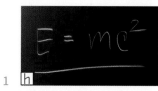 1 [h]

 2 ☐

 3 ☐

 4 ☐

 5 ☐

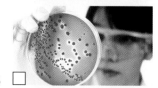 6 ☐

 7 ☐

 8 ☐

 9 ☐

B 🎧 Complete the chart with the correct school subjects. Then listen and check your answers.

Arts	Math	Science	Social studies
art			

C PAIR WORK Which school subjects are or were easy for you? Which are or were difficult? Tell your partner.

"History and music were easy subjects for me, but algebra was difficult!"

2 Language in context Busy schedules

A 🎧 Listen to three people talk about their schedules. Who doesn't have a job?

I'm a high school student. I love history and world geography. I have a part-time job, too. My parents own a restaurant, so I work there on Saturdays. I guess I'm pretty busy. –Kenji

I'm a full-time student. I want to be a doctor. I'm taking six classes and preparing for my medical school entrance exams. I study biology and chemistry every night. –Jan

I'm really busy! I work full-time at a bank. I'm also taking an English class at night with my friend Ricardo. Actually, I'm going to class now. I think I'm late! –Amelia

B What about you? Do you have a busy schedule? What do you do in a typical week?

3 Grammar 🎧 Simple present vs. present continuous

Use the simple present to describe routines and permanent situations.
Kenji **works** on Saturdays.
Jan **studies** every night.
Kenji's parents **own** a restaurant.

Use the present continuous to describe actions in progress or temporary situations.
Amelia **is going** to class right now.
Jan **is preparing** for her medical school entrance exams.
Amelia and Ricardo **are taking** an English class together.

Verbs not usually used in continuous tenses	
believe	mean
have	own
hope	remember
know	seem
like	understand
love	want

A Complete the conversations with the simple present or present continuous forms of the verbs. Then practice with a partner.

1 A _____Are_____ you _____taking_____ (take) a lot of classes these days?

  B I _____ (take) just two: world geography and physics. I _____ (have) a full-time job, so I _____ (not / have) a lot of free time.

2 A How often _____ you _____ (go) to the library?

  B I _____ (go) every Saturday. But I _____ (study) at home a lot, too.
  I _____ (prepare) for an important exam.

3 A How _____ (be) your English class?

  B It _____ (be) fine. I _____ (like) English and _____ (want) to improve my speaking. But we _____ (be) only in the first lesson!

4 A What _____ the teacher _____ (do) now?

  B She _____ (help) some students. They _____ (ask) her questions.
  They _____ (seem) confused about something.

B PAIR WORK Ask and answer the questions in Part A. Answer with your own information.

4 Speaking School and work

A PAIR WORK Read the list. Add one set of questions about school or work.

- What's your favorite class? Are you learning anything interesting?
- Do you have a job? If so, what do you do?
- Are you studying for any exams? Do you study alone or with others?
- What job do you want someday? Are you doing anything to prepare for it?
- Why are you studying English? What do you hope to do in this class?
- _____? _____?

B GROUP WORK Share any interesting information from Part A.

5 Keep talking!

Go to page 123 for more practice.

I can ask and talk about routines. ✓

5

B You're not allowed to . . .

1 **Interactions** Prohibition and obligation

A Do you always follow rules? Do you ever break rules? If so, when?

B 🎧 Listen to the conversation. What *can* students do in the class? Then practice the conversation.

Justin   Excuse me. Do you mind if I sit here?

Fei   Not at all. Go ahead.

Justin   Thanks. I'm Justin, by the way.

Fei   Hi. I'm Fei. Are you new in this class?

Justin   Yeah. Today is my first day. Hey, can we drink coffee in class?

Fei   No. You can't eat or drink in class. It's one of the rules.

Justin   Really? Good to know.

Fei   Oh, and there's another rule. You have to turn off your cell phone.

Justin   OK. Thanks for letting me know.

Fei   Sure. Do you want to be my language partner today? We can choose our speaking partners in this class.

Justin   OK. Thanks.

C 🎧 Read the expressions below. Complete each box with a similar expression from the conversation. Then listen and check your answers.

Expressing prohibition
You can't . . .
(You're not allowed to . . .)
(You're not permitted to . . .)

Expressing obligation
_____
(You need to . . .)
(You must . . .)

D **PAIR WORK** Look at the common signs. Say the rules. Take turns.

"You're not permitted to park here."

2 Listening First day at work

A 🎧 Listen to Joel's co-workers explain the office rules on his first day at work. Number the pictures from 1 to 6.

B 🎧 Listen again. Write the office rules.

1 _____   4 _____
2 _____   5 _____
3 _____   6 _____

3 Speaking Class rules

A **PAIR WORK** Make a list of five important rules for your class like the one below.

Class rules

1. You must raise your hand to speak.
2. You can't send or read text messages.
3. You have to turn off your cell phone.
4. You're not permitted to chew gum.
5. You're allowed to sit anywhere you want.

B **GROUP WORK** Compare your list with another pair. Choose the five most important rules.

C **CLASS ACTIVITY** Share your lists. Can you and your teacher agree on a list of class rules?

I can express prohibition and obligation. ✓

C My behavior

1 Vocabulary Feelings and emotions

A 🎧 Match the words and the pictures. Then listen and check your answers.

a	angry	c	hungry	e	lonely	g	scared	i	thirsty
b	busy	d	jealous	f	nervous	h	sleepy	j	upset

B **PAIR WORK** Why do you think the people in the pictures feel the way they do? Discuss your ideas.

2 Conversation Feeling nervous

A 🎧 Listen to the conversation. Why is Nate eating so late?

Nate Hello?

Laura Hi, Nate. It's Laura. Are you busy?

Nate Not really. I'm just eating some ice cream.

Laura Really? Why are you eating so late?

Nate Oh, I have an exam tomorrow, and I'm kind of nervous about it. I eat when I'm nervous. I'm not even hungry! It's not good, I know.

Laura Well, a lot of people eat when they're nervous. If I'm nervous about something, I just try not to think about it.

Nate That's easier said than done! But what do you do if you have a really important exam?

Laura I study a lot, of course!

B 🎧 Listen to the rest of the conversation. Why did Laura call Nate?

3 Grammar 🎧 Zero conditional

> *Zero conditional sentences describe things that are generally true. Use the simple present for both the* if *clause (the condition) and the main clause.*
>
> What **do** you **do** if you **have** a really important exam?
>> If I **have** a really important exam, I **study** a lot.
>> I **study** a lot if I **have** a really important exam.
>
> *You can usually substitute* when *for* if *in zero conditional sentences.*
>
> **If** I'm nervous about something, I just try not to think about it.
>
> **When** I'm nervous about something, I just try not to think about it.

A Match the conditions and the main clauses. Then compare with a partner.

1 If I'm nervous before an exam, _____
2 When I'm busy with chores at home, _____
3 If I wake up and feel hungry, _____
4 When I get angry at someone, _____
5 If my friends don't call me for a few days, _____
6 When I feel sleepy on Sunday mornings, _____

a. I ask a family member to do some.
b. I start to get lonely.
c. I have something healthy, like an apple.
d. I usually don't say anything to him or her.
e. I like to stay in bed.
f. I take a deep breath and try to relax.

B `PAIR WORK` **Make true sentences about your behavior with the conditions in Part A. Tell your partner.**

"If I'm nervous before an exam, I study with a friend."

4 Pronunciation Stress and rhythm

A 🎧 **Listen and repeat. Notice how stressed words occur with a regular rhythm.**

When I'm **lonely**, I **like** to **chat** or **talk** on the **phone** with my **friends**.

B `PAIR WORK` **Practice the sentences from Exercise 3A. Pay attention to your stress and rhythm.**

5 Speaking Different behaviors

`GROUP WORK` **Read the list. Add two more questions with** *if* **or** *when*. **Then ask and answer them.**

- What do you do if you feel sleepy in class?
- What do you do when you get jealous?
- How do you feel when you're alone at night?
- How do you feel when you speak English in class?
- _____
- _____

6 Keep talking!

`Go to page 124 for more practice.`

I can ask and talk about feelings and reactions. ✓

D Education controversy

Reading 🎧

A Do you think video games can be educational? Why or why not?

B Read the article. What do many parents feel about video games?

Are video games educational?

Many parents have a bad feeling about video games. Some believe that if they allow their children to play video games, they won't do well in school. Others feel that too many video games, especially violent ones, make children feel angry and nervous. If their kids spend a lot of time playing games alone, some parents are afraid that they will feel lonely and have a hard time making friends.

But recent studies suggest a more positive side to video games, and that video games are helping students to learn, to make friends and to build important skills.

One of the biggest advantages of playing video games is that they give the brain a great workout. Every gamer knows that when you are playing video games, you have to think fast and make decisions quickly. In some really hard games, players have to learn how to form strategies, plan their actions and manage their time. Studies also show that many video games are helping students to improve math and reading skills.

Video games can also bring students together and help them make friends. In multiplayer games, players must work with their team to achieve a goal. Some games give players a chance to be leaders and increase their confidence.

Physically, scientists believe that video games may help to manage stress, improve eyesight and increase hand-eye coordination.

In many ways, video games are helping to make learning new skills more fun. Perhaps someday, video games will be a bigger part of a student's education.

C Read the article again. Complete the chart by listing three skills that video games can help students build in each area.

Cognitive (Thinking) Skills	Social skills	Physical skills
improve time management skills	learn to work with a team	

D PAIR WORK What kind of video games do you think are educational? Do you think video games can be played in classrooms? Tell your partner.

2 Listening Is homeschooling for you?

A 🎧 Listen to Julie and her parents discuss homeschooling. What do they like about it, and what are their challenges? Check (✓) the correct answers.

	Likes	Challenges	Advice
Julie	☐ the classroom ☐ the hours ☐ the teachers	☐ texting friends ☐ not seeing friends in class ☐ being in a real school	
Julie's parents	☐ teaching together ☐ choosing the curriculum ☐ working at home	☐ scheduling ☐ giving grades ☐ knowing every subject	

B 🎧 Listen again. What advice do Julie and her parents give to people considering homeschooling? Complete the chart with their advice.

3 Writing Distance education

A PAIR WORK Read the definition of distance education. Then make a list of its advantages and disadvantages.

> Distance education is a type of education where students work on their own at home and communicate with teachers and other students using email, message boards, instant messaging, video chats, and other forms of computer-based communication.

B Do you think learning English by distance education is a good idea or a bad idea? Write a paragraph to explain your opinion. Use the model and your list from Part A.

Advantages of Distance Education

I think learning English by distance education is a very good idea. There are many advantages. For example, students can work at their own speed. This is good for people with full-time jobs or people who can't go to regular classes . . .

C PAIR WORK Compare your ideas.

4 Speaking Advantages and disadvantages

A GROUP WORK What are the advantages and disadvantages of these types of learning? Discuss your ideas.

large classes	private lessons with a tutor	studying abroad
small classes	online learning	watching movies in English

B CLASS ACTIVITY How do you prefer to learn? What type of learning is the most popular?

I can discuss advantages and disadvantages. ✓

Wrap-up

1 Quick pair review

Lesson A Do you remember?

Cross out the word that doesn't belong. Then write the category.
You have two minutes.

1	math	algebra	~~history~~	geometry
2	_____	art	history	world geography
3	_____	music	art	algebra
4	_____	biology	geometry	chemistry

Lesson B Guess!

Think of a place that has rules. Tell your partner things you can and can't do there, but don't say the name of the place. Can your partner guess it? You have two minutes.

A: You're not permitted to talk. You must turn off your cell phone.

B: Is it a library?

Lesson C Find out!

What is one thing both you and your partner do in each situation?
You have three minutes.

- What do you do if you feel scared?
- What do you do if you get a phone call in class?
- What do you do if you have a lot of homework?

A: If I'm scared, I turn on the lights. Do you?

B: No. I lock the doors if I'm scared. Do you?

A: Yes.

Lesson D Give your opinion!

What are two advantages and two disadvantages of taking a class online?
You have three minutes.

2 In the real world

What is a multi-age classroom? Go online and find information in English about one. Then write about it.

- What ages or grades are in the classroom?
- What are some advantages? What are some disadvantages?

A Multi-Age Classroom

At Ambuehl Elementary School, first-, second-, and third-graders are in the same classroom. One advantage is that younger students learn from older students. Another advantage is that . . .

2 Personal stories

Lesson A
- Sentence adverbs
- Past continuous vs. simple past

Lesson B
- Announcing news
- Closing a conversation

Lesson C
- Verbs to describe reactions
- Participial adjectives

Lesson D
- Reading: "Embarrassing Experiences"
- Writing: An embarrassing moment

Warm Up

A Look at the pictures. Which story would you like to hear? Rank them from 1 (very much) to 6 (not much).

B Do you prefer to tell stories about yourself or hear stories about other people? Why?

13

A What were you doing?

1 Vocabulary Sentence adverbs

A 🎧 Match the pictures and the sentences. Then listen and check your answers.

1   2   3   4

_____ **Amazingly**, she came home last night.

_____ **Fortunately**, she was very healthy.

_____ **Sadly**, my cat disappeared last year.

_____ **Strangely**, she had on a little sweater.

5   6   7   8

_____ **Luckily**, someone found it.

_____ **Suddenly**, I realized I didn't have it.

_____ **Surprisingly**, she brought it to my home.

_____ **Unfortunately**, I lost my wallet yesterday.

B **PAIR WORK** Use sentence adverbs to describe incidents that happened to you or people you know. Tell your partner.

"Amazingly, my brother passed his physics exam last week. He didn't study at all!"

2 Language in context Lights out!

A 🎧 Listen to two people describe what they were doing when the power went out last night. What did they do after the power went out?

I was cooking pasta when suddenly everything went dark. Luckily, I had some candles. I couldn't finish making my meal, so I just ate cereal for dinner.

– *Angela*

While my friends and I were watching a movie at home, the lights went out. Unfortunately, no one knew how the movie ended. So, we took turns telling our own endings.

– *Tetsu*

B What about you? Have you ever been in a blackout? What did you do?

3 Grammar 🎧 Past continuous vs. simple past

> Use the past continuous to describe an action in progress in the past.
>
> Angela **was cooking** pasta last night.   Tetsu and his friends **were watching** a movie.
>
> Use the simple past for an event that interrupts that action in progress.
>
> Angela **was cooking** pasta when everything **went** dark.
>
> While Tetsu and his friends **were watching** a movie, the lights **went** out.

A Complete the conversations with the past continuous or simple past forms of the verbs. Then practice with a partner.

1 A What _____were_____ you
      _____doing_____ (do) last night when the
      storm _____ (begin)?
   B I _____ (use) my computer.
      While I _____ (write) my report,
      the electricity suddenly _____
      (go) off.
   A _____ you _____
      (lose) your work?
   B Yeah. Unfortunately, I _____
      (need) to do it again.

2 A How _____ you
      _____ (break) your foot?
   B Oh, I _____ (ski).
   A Really? _____ it
      _____ (hurt)?
   B Of course! But fortunately, someone
      _____ (call) an ambulance.
   A That's good.
   B Yeah, and while I _____ (wait),
      my friends _____ (bring) me
      hot chocolate.

B PAIR WORK Ask and answer questions about what you were doing at the times below.

7:00 this morning   10:00 last night   4:30 yesterday afternoon   this time yesterday

4 Pronunciation Intonation in complex sentences

🎧 **Listen and repeat. Notice how each clause has its own intonation pattern.**

Angela was cooking pasta when everything went dark.

When everything went dark, Angela was cooking pasta.

5 Speaking Story time

GROUP WORK **Complete a sentence below with your own idea. Your group adds sentences with adverbs to create a story. Take turns.**

● I was talking to my best friend when . . .
● I was sleeping one night when . . .
● I was walking down the street when . . .
● I was checking my messages when . . .

A: I was talking to my best friend when my phone rang.

B: Strangely, it was a phone number I didn't know.

C: Luckily, I answered the phone because it was . . .

6 Keep talking!

Go to page 125 for more practice.

I can describe what was happening in the past. ☑️   15

B Guess what!

1 Interactions Sharing news

A Think about different people you know. Do you have any news about them?

B 🎧 Listen to the conversation. What news is Diana sharing?
Then practice the conversation.

Ruben	Hi, Diana. How are you?
Diana	I'm fine. Guess what!
Ruben	What?
Diana	Do you remember Joe from our photography class?
Ruben	Joe? Oh, yeah. Is he OK?
Diana	Oh, he's fine. It's just that he got into film school in Los Angeles. He wants to be a director.
Ruben	Really? Good for him.
Diana	Yeah. I hear he really likes it.
Ruben	That's fantastic!
Diana	Yeah. Hey, I need to get going. I'm late for work.
Ruben	Oh, OK. I'll call you later.

C 🎧 Read the expressions below. Complete each box with a similar expression from the conversation. Then listen and check your answers.

Announcing news

_____

Did you hear what happened?

You'll never guess what happened!

Closing a conversation

_____

Listen, I've got to run.

Sorry, I have to go.

D PAIR WORK Have conversations like the one in Part B. Use these ideas.

Your classmate Lucy Kim moved away. She moved to Spain to study art.

Your teacher Bill Jones got married. He married his girlfriend from high school.

Your friend Pedro Garcia was on TV. He was on a game show and won!

2 Listening You'll never guess!

A 🎧 Listen to Michael and Wendy talk about four different people they know. Number the people from 1 to 4 in the order they talk about them. There is one extra person.

☐ a classmate   ☐ a co-worker   ☐ a family member   ☐ a neighbor   ☐ a teacher

B 🎧 Listen again. Check (✓) the true sentences. Correct the false ones.

1 ☐ Greg is graduating from middle school.

2 ☐ Eva bought a brand-new red car.

3 ☐ Mr. Landers is going to teach a new class.

4 ☐ Cathy is going to be in the school play.

3 Speaking Celebrity news

A **PAIR WORK** Think of four famous people. What is some interesting news about them? Complete the chart.

	Famous person	News
1		
2		
3		
4		

B **CLASS ACTIVITY** Announce your news about the famous people to a classmate. Then close the conversation and talk to another classmate.

C **CLASS ACTIVITY** Who heard the most interesting news?

I can announce news. ✓

I can close a conversation. ✓

C I was really frightened!

1 Vocabulary Verbs to describe reactions

A 🎧 Match the words and the pictures. Then listen and check your answers.

a	amuse	c	confuse	e	embarrass	g	frighten
b	challenge	d	disgust	f	excite	h	interest

 1

 2

 3

 4

 5

 6

 7

 8

B **PAIR WORK** What amuses you? Challenges you? Confuses you? Etc.
Tell your partner.

2 Conversation Around the campfire

A 🎧 Listen to the conversation. What frightened Paul?

David . . . and that's what was on the floor!

Jim Yuck! That story was disgusting!

Paul Well, listen to this. I was watching a movie at home one
night when I heard a strange noise outside the window.

David What did you do?

Paul I was really frightened! I was watching a horror movie,
and I was sitting in the dark. Anyway, I walked to the
window, opened the curtains, and saw a face!

Jim No way! That's frightening!

Paul Not really. It was just my roommate.

David Your roommate?

Paul Yeah. Unfortunately, he lost his key and couldn't get in
the house. He was really embarrassed!

B 🎧 Listen to the rest of the conversation. How did Paul's
roommate react?

3 Grammar ∩ Participial adjectives

Use present participles (-ing) to describe someone or something that causes a reaction.	*Use past participles (-ed) to describe a person's reaction to someone or something.*
That story was **disgusting**.	I was **disgusted** by that story.
The noise was really **frightening**.	I was really **frightened** by the noise.
His actions were really **embarrassing**.	He was really **embarrassed**.

Circle the correct words. Then compare with a partner.

1 This short story is very **challenging** / **challenged**. There's a lot of difficult vocabulary.

2 I'm really **exciting** / **excited** to hear about your trip. Tell me all about it!

3 I liked your story, but I'm **confusing** / **confused** by the ending. Can you explain it?

4 I think my neighbor's stories about her life are very **amusing** / **amused**.

5 I never feel **frightening** / **frightened** when people tell me ghost stories.

6 That joke wasn't funny at all. It was **disgusting** / **disgusted**.

7 That movie was **boring** / **bored**. It wasn't **interesting** / **interested** at all.

8 I'm **surprising** / **surprised** you were **embarrassing** / **embarrassed** by my story.

4 Listening Is that really true?

A ∩ **Listen to Mark's story. Check (✓) the two adjectives that best describe it.**

☐ challenging   ☐ frightening   ☐ disgusting   ☐ amusing

B ∩ **Listen again. Answer the questions.**

1 What are Mark and his friend doing in the tent? _____

2 What did they first hear outside the tent? _____

3 What did Mark's friend want to do? _____

4 What did the voice outside the tent say? _____

5 Speaking My own experience

A **Think about your own experiences. Choose one of the topics from the list below. Then take notes to prepare to talk about it.**

an exciting day	a frightening experience
a confusing moment	an amusing situation
a challenging situation	an interesting conversation

B **PAIR WORK** Tell your partner about your experience. Ask and answer questions for more information.

6 Keep talking!

Go to page 126 for more practice.

I can tell personal stories. ✓

19

D How embarrassing!

1 Reading 🎧

A How do you react when you feel embarrassed? Do you turn red? Do you get angry if people laugh at you?

B Read the article. Where did each person's embarrassing moment happen?

C ↻ 🔍 🏠

STUDENT TIMES

Home	Metro ⌄	Sports ⌄	Opinions ⌄	Arts ⌄	Photos	Videos	Search

Embarrassing Experiences
By Jack Preston

Last week, *Student Times* reporter Jack Preston asked students, "What's the most embarrassing experience you've ever had?" Here are five of his favorite responses.

This happened at work a few years ago. I was on an elevator, and a man got on that I didn't know. He asked, "How are you?" I answered, "Pretty good." Then he asked, "What's new?" and I said, "Nothing much." Finally, he turned and said, "Do you mind?" He was on his cell phone! I was so embarrassed! ☐ – **Susan**

I sing all the time. One time, a few years ago, I was singing in the shower when my sister came into the bathroom and recorded me! Later, we were driving, and my sister put on some music. ☐ It was me! I was really embarrassed and turned bright red. – **Becky**

I fell asleep in math class once. I closed my eyes for a second, and the next thing I remember is my teacher's voice. He was asking me a question. When I didn't answer, he walked over to my desk. He asked the question again. ☐ – **Alex**

My friend's parents had a birthday party for her at their new house last year. They had these glass doors that went out to the backyard. We were all outside, and I had to use the restroom. So I was running to the house and then – BAM! I hit the glass doors. I was really confused for a minute. I thought they were open, but they were closed! ☐ – **Anita**

When I was in middle school, I bought this cool new sweater. I wore it to a school dance the next evening, and everyone laughed at me when I came in. The sweater was inside out! So I went into the restroom to change and came back out. ☐ Everyone laughed at me again. – **Evan**

C Read the article again. Write the numbers of the missing sentences in the correct paragraphs.

1 Luckily, I knew the answer.
2 Fortunately, the doors opened, and I got off.
3 Unfortunately, it was now on backwards!
4 Suddenly, she started to laugh.
5 Amazingly, I wasn't hurt at all.

D **PAIR WORK** Whose story do you think is the most embarrassing? Discuss your ideas.

2 Writing An embarrassing moment

A Think of an embarrassing moment that happened to you or someone you know. Answer the questions.

- When did it happen? _____
- Where did it happen? _____
- Who was there? _____
- Why was it embarrassing? _____

B Write a description of an embarrassing moment that happened to you or someone you know. Use the model and your answers in Part A to help you.

Embarrassed at the Supermarket

When I was about six years old, I was at the supermarket with my mom. She was shopping for groceries. I wanted some candy, but my mom didn't want to buy me any. So, when my mother wasn't looking, I took some candy and put it into the cart. The problem was that I put the candy into the wrong cart . . .

C **CLASS ACTIVITY** Post your papers around the classroom. Then read the stories and rate them from 1 (very embarrassing) to 4 (not embarrassing at all). Which stories are the most embarrassing?

3 Speaking It happened to me!

A Imagine you are the person in one of these pictures. Take notes to prepare to tell the story.

B **GROUP WORK** Tell your stories. Ask and answer questions for more information.

A: I was having dinner with my wife. We were at a restaurant and I accidentally went into the ladies' restroom instead of the men's restroom.

B: Oh, no! What did you do?

I can describe embarrassing moments. ✓

21

Wrap-up

1 Quick pair review

Lesson A `Brainstorm!`

Make a list of sentence adverbs. How many do you know? You have one minute.

Lesson B `Do you remember?`

Complete the expressions with the correct words to announce news and close a conversation. You have one minute.

1 Did you hear _____?
2 You'll _____ what happened!
3 Guess _____!
4 Listen, I've _____ run!
5 Hey, I need to _____.
6 Sorry, I _____ to go.

Lesson C `Test your partner!`

Say four present or past participles. Can your partner use them correctly in a sentence? Take turns. You have two minutes.

A: Disgusting.

B: In my opinion, hamburgers are disgusting!

Lesson D `Find out!`

What are two things both you and your partner do when you are embarrassed? You have one minute.

A: When I'm embarrassed, I laugh a lot. Do you?

B: No, I don't. I turn red, though. Do you?

A: Yes, my cheeks turn red, too!

2 In the real world

Go online and find an embarrassing, interesting, or amusing story in English about a famous person. Then write about it.

Beyoncé's Embarrassing Moment

Beyoncé had an embarrassing experience at a concert. She was walking down the stairs on stage when she tripped and fell. Luckily, she didn't get hurt. Actually, she got up and continued to sing! . . .

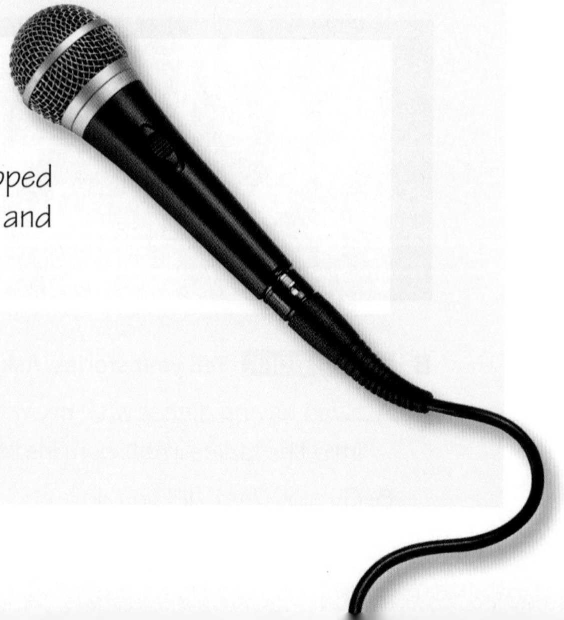

Style and fashion

Lesson A
- Fashion statements
- *Used to*

Lesson B
- Asking where things are
- Asking for an alternative

Lesson C
- Clothing styles
- Defining relative clauses

Lesson D
- Reading: "Dress to Impress"
- Writing: Class survey

Warm Up

A Describe the pictures. What are the people doing?

B Which styles do you like? Which don't you like? Why?

A Fashion trends

1 Vocabulary Fashion statements

A 🎧 Complete the chart with the correct words. Then listen and check your answers.

a bracelet

contact lenses

dyed hair

earrings

glasses

high heels

a leather jacket

a ponytail

sandals

a uniform

Shoes	Clothing	Eyewear	Hairstyles	Jewelry

B **PAIR WORK** Which things in Part A do you wear or have? Tell your partner.

2 Language in context Fashion history

A 🎧 Read about three fashions from the past. Who wore each fashion?

Togas Two thousand years ago, Roman men used to wear sandals and a long piece of clothing called a toga.

Wigs In the seventeenth and eighteenth centuries, rich men and women in England and France used to wear long wigs. Some of the wigs had ponytails.

Leather jackets In the 1950s, many American men used to wear leather jackets with jeans. Before that time, most teenagers didn't use to wear jeans.

B Do people still wear the fashions from Part A today? If so, how are they similar or different?

3 Grammar 🎧 *Used to*

> Used to *refers to something that was true in the past but isn't anymore or something that happened regularly in the past but doesn't anymore.*
>
> I **used to** have a black leather jacket.
>
> Men and women in England and France **used to** wear long wigs.
>
> **Did** you **use to** dye your hair?
>
>   Yes, I **used to** dye my hair all the time, but I don't dye it anymore.
>
>   No, I **didn't use to** dye my hair, but I do now.

A Write sentences with *used to* (✓) or *didn't use to* (✗). Then compare with a partner.

1 Max / (✓) dye his hair black   Max used to dye his hair black.

2 Carly / (✗) wear a uniform to school   _____

3 Tina and I / (✓) have ponytails   _____

4 Britney / (✓) wear the same bracelet every day   _____

5 Roberto and Ana / (✗) wear glasses   _____

6 Kendra /(✗) like leather skirts   _____

B `PAIR WORK` Complete the sentences with true information. Tell your partner.

1 I used to _____ as a kid, but I don't now.

2 I didn't use to _____, but some of my friends did.

3 Lots of people used to _____, but they don't now.

4 Pronunciation *Used to* and *use to*

🎧 Listen and repeat. Notice how *used to* and *use to* sound the same.

/yustə/
I **used to** wear a uniform.

/yustə/
I didn't **use to** dye my hair, but I do now.

5 Speaking Past and present

A `PAIR WORK` Read the list. Add two more questions about style and fashion. Then interview your partner. Take notes.

● What kind of clothing did you use to wear?

● What kind of hairstyles did you use to have?

● What's something you didn't use to wear but do now?

● _____

● _____

B `PAIR WORK` Tell another classmate any interesting information about your partner's style and fashion.

6 Keep talking!

Student A go to page 127 and
Student B go to page 128 for more practice.

I can ask about and describe past fashions. ✓

B Does this come in...?

1 Interactions Shopping questions

A Where do you like to shop for clothes? What kinds of clothes do you like?

B 🎧 Listen to the conversations. What size does Jenny want? Then practice the conversations.

Jenny	Excuse me.
Salesclerk 1	Yes?
Jenny	Where are the raincoats?
Salesclerk 1	They're on the second floor, in Outerwear.
Jenny	Thank you.

Jenny	Excuse me.
Salesclerk 2	Can I help you?
Jenny	Yes. Does this come in a medium?
Salesclerk 2	I believe so. Let's see... Yes, here you go.
Jenny	Thank you.
Salesclerk 2	If you want to try it on, the fitting rooms are over there.

C 🎧 Read the expressions below. Complete each box with a similar expression from the conversations. Then listen and check your answers.

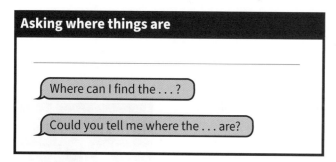

Asking where things are

_____

> Where can I find the ...?

> Could you tell me where the ... are?

Asking for an alternative

_____

> Do you have this in ...?

> Can I get this in ...?

D **PAIR WORK** Have conversations like the ones in Part B. Use these items.

2 Listening Shopping for clothes

A 🎧 Listen to four customers shopping in a clothing store. Number the items they discuss from 1 to 4. There are two extra items.

☐ ☐ ☐ ☐ ☐ ☐

B 🎧 Listen again. Does each customer ask the salesclerk for the location or an alternative of the item? Write L (location) or A (alternative).

1 _____ 2 _____ 3 _____ 4 _____

3 Speaking In a department store

GROUP WORK Role-play the situation. Then change roles.

Student A: You are a salesclerk in a department store. Student B is shopping for a particular item. Direct Student B to the correct section of the store. Use the picture to help you.

Student B: You are shopping in a department store. Students A and C are salesclerks. Ask Student A where a particular clothing item is. Then ask Student C for a different item.

Student C: You are a salesclerk in a department store. Student B is shopping for a particular item in your section of the store. Help Student B get a different item.

A: *Good afternoon. Can I help you?*

B: *Yes. Where can I find women's shoes?*

A: *On the second floor, in Footwear.*

DIRECTORY

3rd Floor
- MEN'S FASHION
- CHILDREN'S FASHION
- ACTIVE & SWIM
- RESTAURANT

2nd Floor
- WOMEN'S FASHION
- FOOTWEAR
- SLEEPWEAR
- PERSONAL STYLIST

1st Floor
- JEWELRY
- HANDBAGS
- SUNGLASSES
- OUTERWEAR
- BEAUTY
- CONCIERGE

I can ask where something is in a store. ✅

I can ask for a specific product. ✅

C The latest look

1 Vocabulary Clothing styles

A 🎧 Write the correct adjectives to describe the clothing. Then listen and check your answers.

fashionable
✓ flashy
glamorous
old-fashioned

1 _____flashy_____
2 _____
3 _____
4 _____

retro
tacky
trendy
✓ weird

5 _____weird_____
6 _____
7 _____
8 _____

B PAIR WORK Which styles do you like? Which don't you like? Why? Tell your partner.

2 Conversation People-watching

A 🎧 Listen to the conversation. What does Ryan think of the man's tie?

Ryan   Look at that woman's jacket!

Jill   Wow! It's pretty flashy. I definitely think she's someone who likes to stand out in a crowd.

Ryan   I know what you mean. I like clothes which don't attract a lot of attention.

Jill   Really?

Ryan   Yeah. I usually shop for clothes that are simple and inexpensive. Hey, check out that guy's tie. Talk about old-fashioned!

Jill   Do you think so? Actually, I think it's pretty fashionable. It's kind of retro.

Ryan   Well, I'd never wear anything like that.

B 🎧 Listen to the rest of the conversation. How does Jill describe her style?

3 Grammar 🎧 Defining relative clauses

> *Defining relative clauses specify which or what kind of people or things you are describing.*
>
> *Use* that *or* who *for people.* | *Use* that *or* which *for things.*
>
> I'm a person **that** loves flashy clothes. | I shop for clothes **that** are simple and inexpensive.
>
> She's someone **who** likes to stand out in a crowd. | He likes clothes **which** don't attract a lot of attention.

A Complete each sentence with *that, who,* or *which*. Then compare with a partner.

1 I prefer salesclerks _____ are honest with me.

2 I'm the kind of person _____ rarely follows fashion.

3 I hardly ever wear clothes _____ are trendy.

4 I know someone _____ loves expensive clothes.

5 Some of my friends wear stuff _____ is a little too weird.

6 I usually buy clothes _____ are on sale.

7 I'm someone _____ likes reading fashion magazines.

8 I buy shoes _____ go with lots of different clothing.

B **PAIR WORK** Make the sentences in Part A true for you. Tell your partner.

A: I prefer salesclerks who don't say anything. I know what looks good on me.

B: Not me. I need all the help I can get!

4 Speaking Thoughts on fashion

A Complete the sentences with your own ideas.

1 I really don't like clothes that are _____ .

2 _____ is a word which describes my personal style.

3 When shopping, I like friends who _____ .

4 _____ is a person who always looks fashionable.

5 I think _____ is a color that looks good on me.

6 A _____ is something that I never wear.

7 _____ is a designer who's very popular now.

B **GROUP WORK** Compare your ideas. Ask and answer questions for more information.

A: I really don't like clothes that are expensive.

B: Really? I only like expensive clothes!

C: I like clothes that are comfortable.

5 Keep talking!

Go to page 129 for more practice.

I can express opinions about style and fashion. ✓

29

D Views on fashion

1 Reading 🎧

A What's in style these days? Do you like the current fashions for men and women?

B Read the article. Do you find any of the information surprising?

DRESS TO IMPRESS

Image is important to many people, but what do men and women really think of each other's fashion choices? What do people actually think looks good on the opposite sex? Are you dressing to impress your target audience? What are some clothing items that you should invest in to get someone's attention?

Fashion styles like "artsy," for the more creative crowd, or vintage, for a touch of the past, or even fancy "chic" clothing may show a little of your personality. But it doesn't always mean that the person you may be trying to impress *will be* impressed.

It may be simpler than you think! Women generally like men that look like they have made an effort. As for men, they seem to be the opposite! Here is what most men and women say that they prefer:

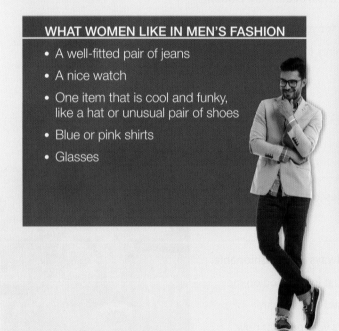

WHAT WOMEN LIKE IN MEN'S FASHION
- A well-fitted pair of jeans
- A nice watch
- One item that is cool and funky, like a hat or unusual pair of shoes
- Blue or pink shirts
- Glasses

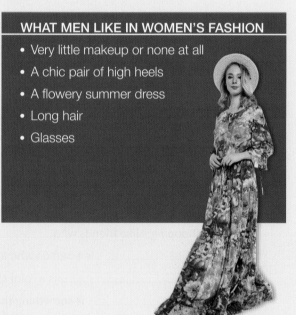

WHAT MEN LIKE IN WOMEN'S FASHION
- Very little makeup or none at all
- A chic pair of high heels
- A flowery summer dress
- Long hair
- Glasses

C Read the article again. Are the sentences true or false? Write T (true) or F (false).

1 Most women like to wear well-fitted jeans with a blue shirt. _____
2 Both men and women like it when the other wears glasses. _____
3 You have to dress very chic if you want to attract a man. _____
4 Guys often think "less is more" for a woman. _____
5 Many guys like it when a woman wears high heels. _____
6 Most guys think women look nice with long hair. _____

D PAIR WORK Do you agree with the information in the article? Why or why not? Discuss your ideas.

2 **Listening** An interview with Eduardo

A 🎧 **Listen to an interview with Eduardo, a fashion designer. Number the questions from 1 to 5 in the order you hear them. Write the numbers in the boxes.**

☐ Are high heels old-fashioned? _____

☐ Should belts and shoes be the same color? _____

☐ Does black go with everything? _____

☐ Is it OK for men to wear earrings? _____

☐ Can guys wear pink? _____

B 🎧 **Listen again. How does Eduardo answer each question? Write Y (yes) or N (no) on each line.**

C **Do you agree with Eduardo's opinions? Why or why not?**

3 **Writing and speaking** Class survey

A **GROUP WORK** **Create a survey with four questions about fashion and style. Use the topics below or your own ideas.**

cool places to shop	popular colors
current clothing styles	the latest gadgets
current hairstyles	trendy accessories
popular brands	unpopular colors

Fashion Survey

1. What color is popular right now?
2. What's the most popular brand of jeans?
3. Where is a cool place to buy jewelry?
4. What gadget does everyone want now?

B **CLASS ACTIVITY** **Ask and answer the questions in your surveys. Take notes.**

C **GROUP WORK** **Share and summarize the results.**

Our Class Survey Results

Most people think blue is popular right now. Red was second and green was third. Only a few people think black, orange, or purple are popular. Only one person thinks yellow is popular.

The most popular brand of jeans is Sacco. A lot of people have these. Next was a brand called Durango. These were the only two brands that people mentioned.

Over half of the people in class think Glitter is a cool place to buy jewelry. Some people think the best place to buy jewelry is from people who sell it on the street. Two people . . .

D **CLASS ACTIVITY** **Share your most interesting results. Do you agree with the answers you heard? Give your own opinions.**

Wrap-up

1 Quick pair review

Lesson A `Do you remember?`

Cross out the word that doesn't belong. Then write the category. You have two minutes.

1	_____	high heels	sandals	glasses
2	_____	a bracelet	contact lenses	earrings
3	_____	dyed hair	a uniform	a ponytail
4	_____	a uniform	high heels	a leather jacket
5	_____	glasses	contact lenses	earrings

Lesson B `Brainstorm!`

Make a list of three ways to ask where something is and three ways to ask for an alternative. You have two minutes.

Lesson C `Test your partner!`

Say each pair of sentences. Can your partner make them into one sentence with *which* or *who*? You have two minutes.

Student A

1 I'm a trendy person. I don't like old-fashioned clothes.
2 I usually wear glasses. They aren't glamorous.
3 Julie shops for stuff. It is affordable.

Student B

1 I usually wear hats. They are weird.
2 I know someone. She likes flashy bracelets.
3 Kyle is a guy. He wears tacky clothes.

A: I'm a trendy person. I don't like old-fashioned clothes.

B: I'm a trendy person who doesn't like old-fashioned clothes.

Lesson D `Find out!`

What are two colors that both you and your partner think are good for women to wear? What are two colors you both think are good for guys to wear? You have two minutes.

2 In the real world

What clothes used to be trendy? Go online and find examples of trendy clothes from one decade in the past. Then write about them.

1950s   1960s   1970s   1980s   1990s

Trends in the 1950s

Long dresses used to be popular in the 1950s. Poodle skirts used to be trendy, too. Women used to . . .

4 Interesting lives

Warm Up

A Describe the pictures. What are the people doing?

B Check (✓) the two most interesting activities. Have you ever done them? If not, would you like to try them?

33

A Have you ever been on TV?

1 Vocabulary Experiences

A 🎧 Complete the phrases with the correct words. Then listen and check your answers.

an award	a famous person	on TV	to a new city
a bone	✓ in a play	seasick	your phone

1 act _in a play_

2 be _____

3 break _____

4 get _____

5 lose _____

6 meet _____

7 move _____

8 win _____

B **PAIR WORK** Which experiences in Part A are good to have? Which are not good to have? Discuss your ideas.

"It's good to win an award. It's not good to get seasick."

2 Language in context A local hero

A 🎧 Read Brian's group messages with some friends. Why is Brian excited?

> **Brian** 17:02
> You'll never believe what happened! I'm going to be on the TV news tonight! My first time!

> **Jill** 17:02
> You're kidding! Why?

> **Brian** 17:03
> It's a surprise. You have to watch. Have you ever been on TV?

> **Jill** 17:03
> No, I haven't. One of my friends is an actress, though, and I've seen her on TV a couple of times.

> **Hideo** 17:03
> I've never been on TV, but my sister Kumiko has been on TV lots of times. She's a TV reporter!

B What about you? Would you like to be on TV? Why or why not?

3 Grammar 🎧 Present perfect

> *Use the present perfect to describe events or experiences that happened at an unspecified time in the past. Use* have / has *and the past participle of the verb.*
>
> **Have** you ever **seen** a friend on TV?   **Has** your sister ever **been** on TV?
>   Yes, I **have**.   Yes, she **has**.
>   No, I **haven't**.   No, she **hasn't**.
>
> *Use frequency expressions with the present perfect to give more information.*
>
> I've **never** been on TV.   My sister has been on TV **lots of times**.

A Complete the conversations with the present perfect forms of the verbs. Then practice with a partner.

1 A _____ you ever _____ (be) to another country?

   B Yes, I _____ . I _____ (be) to Brazil.

2 A _____ you ever _____ (eat) sushi?

   B Yes, I _____ . I _____ (have) it many times.

3 A _____ you ever _____ (lose) your wallet?

   B No, I _____ . Luckily, I _____ never _____ (lose) it.

4 A _____ your best friend ever _____ (call) you in the middle of the night?

   B No, she _____ . But I _____ (do) that to her once or twice!

B **PAIR WORK** Ask and answer the questions in Part A. Answer with your own information.

🎧 Regular past participles

act	➡	acted
chat	➡	chatted
try	➡	tried

Irregular past participles

be	➡	been
break	➡	broken
do	➡	done
eat	➡	eaten
go	➡	gone
have	➡	had
lose	➡	lost
meet	➡	met
see	➡	seen
win	➡	won

Turn to page 151 for a list of more past participles.

4 Speaking Yes, I have!

A Complete the questions with your own ideas. Then check (✓) the things you've done, and write down how often you've done them.

Have you ever . . . ?	Me		Name _____		Name _____	
eaten _____	☐		☐		☐	
been _____	☐		☐		☐	
seen _____	☐		☐		☐	
had _____	☐		☐		☐	
won _____	☐		☐		☐	
met _____	☐		☐		☐	

B **GROUP WORK** Interview two classmates. Complete the chart with their answers. Who has had similar experiences?

5 Keep talking!

Go to page 130 for more practice.

I can ask and talk about life experiences. ✓

B What I mean is...

1 Interactions Checking and clarifying meaning

A How often do you eat out? Do you ever cook at home? Do you ever order takeout?

B 🎧 Listen to the conversation. How often does Sam eat out? Then practice the conversation.

Elena	I'm getting hungry.
Sam	Me, too.
Elena	Hey, Sam, there's a great Mexican restaurant near the school. Have you ever tried it?
Sam	No, I haven't. Actually, I don't eat in restaurants.
Elena	Really? Are you saying you never go to restaurants?
Sam	Well, no, not *never*. I mean I just don't eat out very often.
Elena	Why not?
Sam	I'm allergic to certain foods, like peanuts. If I eat them, my skin gets red and itchy.
Elena	That sounds awful!
Sam	It is!

C 🎧 Read the expressions below. Complete each box with a similar expression from the conversation. Then listen and check your answers.

Checking meaning	Clarifying meaning
_____	_____
Do you mean...?	What I mean is,...
Does that mean...?	What I'm saying is,...

D Number the sentences in the conversation from 1 to 7. Then practice with a partner.

_____ **A:** What? Do you mean you never eat pizza?

_____ **A:** I see. So, when can I come over for homemade pizza?

___1___ **A:** I feel a little hungry.

_____ **A:** Have you ever been to Pizza Palace? We can go there.

_____ **B:** So do I.

_____ **B:** No, not *never*. What I mean is, I usually make it myself.

_____ **B:** Actually, I never go to fast-food places.

2 Pronunciation Contrastive stress in responses

A 🎧 **Listen and repeat. Notice how the stressed words emphasize contrast.**

Are you saying you never go to restaurants?

Well, not **never**. I mean I just don't eat out **very often**.

B PAIR WORK **Practice the conversation in Exercise 1D again. Stress words to emphasize contrast.**

3 Listening Why not?

A 🎧 **Listen to four conversations about habits and preferences. Correct the false information.**

1 Danielle ~~often~~ *never* goes to hair salons.
2 Todd loves going to the beach.
3 Jessica always walks to school.
4 Mitch never streams movies.

B 🎧 **Listen again. How do the people explain their habits and preferences? Check (✓) the correct answers.**

1 Danielle's explanation:
   ☐ She finds it too expensive.
   ☐ Her sister cuts her hair.
   ☐ She cuts her own hair.

2 Todd's explanation:
   ☐ It's not easy to get there.
   ☐ He doesn't know how to swim.
   ☐ He doesn't like to be in the sun.

3 Jessica's explanation:
   ☐ The school is only five minutes away.
   ☐ She doesn't have a driver's license.
   ☐ She prefers to walk for the exercise.

4 Mitch's explanation:
   ☐ The movie theater is too far away.
   ☐ He thinks tickets are too expensive.
   ☐ He prefers to stream movies at home.

4 Speaking Unusual habits

A **Write four statements about any unusual or interesting habits and behaviors you have. Use the questions to help you, or think of your own ideas.**

- Is there a food you eat all the time?
- Is there a place you never go?
- Is there someone you talk to every day?
- Is there something you never do?
- Is there an expression you say all the time?

1 _____   3 _____
2 _____   4 _____

B PAIR WORK **Tell your partner about each habit or behavior. Your partner checks the meaning, and you clarify it. Take turns.**

A: *I eat chocolate all the time.*

B: *Does that mean you eat it every day?*

A: *Well, no, not every day. I mean I have chocolate several times a week.*

I can check and clarify meaning. ✓

C Life experiences

1 Vocabulary Fun things to do

A 🎧 Match the phrases and the pictures. Then listen and check your answers.

a climb a mountain	c go camping	e go whale-watching	g try an exotic food
b eat in a fancy restaurant	d go to a spa	f ride a roller coaster	h try an extreme sport

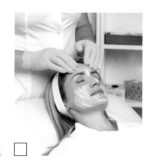 1 ☐

 2 ☐

 3 ☐

 4 ☐

 5 ☐

 6 ☐

 7 ☐

 8 ☐

B PAIR WORK Have you ever done the fun things in Part A? Tell your partner.

2 Conversation A fancy restaurant

A 🎧 Listen to the conversation. Do you think Alice will order frog legs?

Alice   Wow! This place is nice!

Emma   Have you ever eaten in a fancy restaurant before?

Alice   Yes, I have. I've eaten in a few expensive restaurants, but this place is amazing.

Emma   You can try a lot of exotic food here, and all of their dishes are excellent. Oh, look. Tonight's special is frog legs.

Alice   Frog legs? Umm, I don't know. . . .

Emma   Have you ever tried them?

Alice   No, I haven't. But my brother tried them once a few years ago.

Emma   Did he like them?

Alice   I don't think so. He got sick later that night.

B 🎧 Listen to the rest of the conversation. What do Alice and Emma order?

3 Grammar 🎧 Present perfect vs. simple past

> *Use the present perfect to describe events or experiences at an unspecified time in the past.*
>
> **Have** you ever **eaten** in a fancy restaurant?
>   Yes, I **have**. I'**ve eaten** in a few expensive restaurants.
>
> *Use the simple past to describe events or experiences that happened at a specific time in the past.*
>
> Have you ever tried frog legs?
>   No, I haven't. But my brother **tried** them once **a few years ago**.
>
> **Did** he **like** them?
>   I don't think so. He **got** sick later **that night**.

A Complete the conversations with the present perfect or simple past forms of the verbs. Then practice with a partner.

1   A   _____ you ever _____ (see) a whale?

    B   No, I _____. But I _____ always _____ (want) to.

2   A   _____ you _____ (do) anything fun last weekend?

    B   Yes, I _____. I _____ (go) camping with my sister.

3   A   _____ you ever _____ (eat) in a fancy restaurant?

    B   Yes, I _____. I _____ (go) to Lucia's last year.

4   A   What extreme sports _____ you _____ (try)?

    B   I _____ (not / try) any. But my sister _____ (go) skydiving once!

5   A   What _____ you _____ (do) on your last vacation?

    B   My friend and I _____ (go) to a spa.

B **PAIR WORK** Ask and answer the questions in Part A. Answer with your own information.

4 Speaking Is that true?

A Write two true sentences and one false sentence about interesting life experiences you've had.

1 _____

2 _____

3 _____

B **GROUP WORK** Share your sentences. Your group asks you questions and guesses the false sentence. Take turns.

A: I've been to a wrestling match.

B: Really? Who did you go with?

5 Keep talking!

Go to page 131 for more practice.

I can describe details of my experiences. ✓

D What a life!

1 Reading 🎧

A What do you think an astronaut's life is like? What do people need to do or know to become astronauts?

B Read the interview. According to Dr. Pettit, what's the most exciting thing he's experienced?

The life of an ASTRONAUT

Dr. Donald Pettit is a NASA astronaut.

Interviewer:	I'm sure people ask you this question all of the time, Dr. Pettit, but I have to ask it: Have you ever been to space?
Dr. Pettit:	Yes, I have. I was a crew member of *Expedition 6*, and I spent five and a half months at the International Space Station. We call it the ISS.
Interviewer:	How many times have you gone up on the space shuttle?
Dr. Pettit:	I've ridden the space shuttle to the ISS twice.
Interviewer:	And what was the best part about being in space?
Dr. Pettit:	Being able to float. It was the worst part, too.
Interviewer:	Have you visited any other interesting places while working for NASA?
Dr. Pettit:	Well, I lived in Russia for about two years while I was training to fly to the ISS. I've also been to Antarctica.
Interviewer:	Not many people can say that! I understand that you like to work with tools. Have you ever invented anything?
Dr. Pettit:	Yes. During my second trip into space, I made a special coffee cup so we could drink in space, much like we do here on Earth. I just couldn't get used to drinking coffee out of a small bag through a straw!
Interviewer:	I don't think I could get used to that, either. But why did you have to drink coffee that way before?
Dr. Pettit:	Without the bag or my special cup, the coffee floats in space, too.
Interviewer:	Of course! Well, you've accomplished so much, Dr. Pettit. Considering all of it, what's the most exciting thing that you've experienced?
Dr. Pettit:	Seeing the birth of my twin boys.
Interviewer:	Wow, what a life! Thanks so much for sharing, Dr. Pettit.

C Read the interview again. What things has Dr. Pettit done? Check (✓) the correct answers.

- ☐ walked on the moon
- ☐ been to the ISS
- ☐ ridden the space shuttle
- ☐ traveled to Antarctica
- ☐ had twin daughters
- ☐ invented something

D **PAIR WORK** Would you like to travel to space? Why or why not? What would be the most interesting thing about it? Discuss your ideas.

2 Listening A memorable life

A 🎧 **Listen to Leo ask his grandmother about her life. Number the questions from 1 to 5 in the order that you hear them.**

☐ When did you meet Grandpa? _____

☐ What's something interesting you've done? _____

☐ Where else have you lived? _____

☐ Where were you born? _____

☐ Have you been back? _____

B 🎧 **Listen again. Write the grandmother's answers to the questions in Part A.**

3 Writing and speaking Interesting people, places, or things

A **Choose one of the topics. Answer the questions.**

Topics	Questions
A close friend I've had	Who is your friend? How exactly did you meet? Is this person your friend now? Why or why not?
A special place I've been	Where is this place? What made this place so special? Have you ever been back? Why or why not?
An interesting thing I've done	What did you do? How did you feel after doing it? Would you like to do it again? Why or why not?

B **Write a paragraph about your topic. Use the model and your answers in Part A to help you.**

My Friend Lucas

I've had had several good friends, but one that was very special to me was my friend Lucas. He moved into the house next door when I was eight. We became good friends. We walked to school together and always played together at his house. He had a great bike, and I used to ride it. He moved to another city after a year. I've tried to find him online, but haven't had any luck. I . . .

C **PAIR WORK** **Read your partner's paragraph. Write five questions to get more information.**

D **PAIR WORK** **Ask and answer your questions.**

"So, tell me, why did you become friends?"

I can ask and talk about a memorable experience. ✓

Wrap-up

1 Quick pair review

Lesson A Find out!
What is one place both you and your partner have been? One food you both
have tried? One movie you both have seen? You have two minutes.

A: I've been to the art museum downtown. Have you?

B: No, I haven't. I've been to our university library. Have you?

A: Yes, I have.

Lesson B Do you remember?
What can you say to clarify meaning? Check (✓) your answers. You have
one minute.

☐ What I mean is, . . .   ☐ I didn't use to . . .

☐ What time is . . . ?   ☐ I mean . . .

☐ What I'm saying is, . . .   ☐ I used to go . . .

Lesson C Brainstorm!
Imagine you and your partner are going on vacation together. Make a list
of eight fun things to do on your trip. You have two minutes.

Lesson D Guess!
Describe a memorable experience you've had, but don't say where it was.
Can your partner guess where you were? You have two minutes.

2 In the real world

What do you think would be a memorable vacation? Find information in
English online or in a travel magazine about one place. Then write about it.

A Vacation in Hawaii

Hawaii is a good place for a vacation. I've always wanted
to go whale-watching, and I read that you can see whales
in the Pacific Ocean from December to early May. The
best places to see them are Maui, Molokai, and Lanai.

I've also read about Haleakala National Park in Hawaii. A
lot of people climb Mount Haleakala. I've seen pictures of
it. It looks really beautiful. The weather is usually . . .

5 Our world

Lesson A
- Human-made wonders
- Comparisons with adjectives and nouns

Lesson B
- Expressing disbelief
- Saying you don't know

Lesson C
- Geographical features
- Superlatives with adjectives and nouns

Lesson D
- Reading "Seven Wonders of the Natural World"
- Writing: A natural wonder

Burj Khalifa – the U.A.E.

Chichén Itzá – Mexico

Icehotel – Sweden

Cinque Terre – Italy

Yellowstone National Park – the U.S.A.

Kinkaku-ji Temple – Japan

Warm Up

A Look at the pictures. Rank the places you would like to visit from 1 (the most) to 6 (the least).

B Why do you want to visit your top three places?

A Older, taller, and more famous

1 Vocabulary Human-made wonders

A 🎧 Label the pictures with the correct words. Then listen and check your answers.

bridge	plaza	stadium	tower
canal	skyscraper	subway system	tunnel

1 _____

2 _____

3 _____

4 _____

5 _____

6 _____

7 _____

8 _____

B **PAIR WORK** Can you name a famous example for each word? Tell your partner.

"The Panama Canal is very famous."

2 Language in context Two amazing views

A 🎧 Read the question posted on a website for visitors to New York City.
Which view does the site recommend?

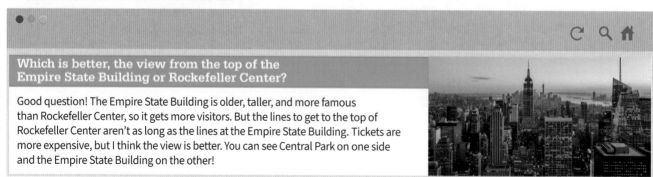

Which is better, the view from the top of the Empire State Building or Rockefeller Center?

Good question! The Empire State Building is older, taller, and more famous than Rockefeller Center, so it gets more visitors. But the lines to get to the top of Rockefeller Center aren't as long as the lines at the Empire State Building. Tickets are more expensive, but I think the view is better. You can see Central Park on one side and the Empire State Building on the other!

B What about you? Where can you go in your town or city for a great view?
Have you ever been there?

3 Grammar 🎧 Comparisons with adjectives and nouns

> *Use the -er ending or* more . . . than *with adjectives to make comparisons.*
> The Empire State Building is **older**, **taller**, and **more famous than** Rockefeller Center.
>
> *You can also use* not as . . . as *to make comparisons with adjectives.*
> The lines at Rockefeller Center are**n't as long as** the lines at the Empire State Building.
> Tickets to the Empire State Building are**n't as expensive as** tickets to Rockefeller Center.
>
> *Use* more . . . than *to make comparisons with nouns.*
> The Empire State Building gets **more visitors than** Rockefeller Center.
> Rockefeller Center has **more observation space than** the Empire State Building.

A Read the information about the Maracanã Stadium and Nissan Stadium. Make comparisons with the adjectives and nouns below. Then compare with a partner.

Maracanã Stadium, Brazil

Year opened: 1950
Seating capacity: 87,101 people
Field size: 88,802 square feet
Height: 105 feet
Number of tiers: 1
Length of construction: 1 year and 10 months

Nissan Stadium, Japan

Year opened: 1998
Seating capacity: 72,327 people
Field size: 82,925 square feet
Height: 170 feet
Number of tiers: 2
Length of construction: 3 years and 9 months

1	(new)	Maracanã Stadium
2	(people)	Maracanã Stadium
3	(big)	Nissan Stadium
4	(tall)	Nissan Stadium
5	(tiers)	Maracanã Stadium
6	(long)	The construction of Maracanã Stadium

1. *isn't as new as Nissan Stadium* _____.
2. _____.
3. _____.
4. _____.
5. _____.
6. _____.

B PAIR WORK Which soccer stadium do you think is more crowded? Why? Discuss your ideas.

4 Speaking Comparisons

PAIR WORK Complete the chart with two examples of each place. Then make comparisons with the adjectives and nouns in the chart.

Places	Example 1	Example 2	Comparisons
cities			people? / exciting?
stadiums			old? / big?
skyscrapers			tall? / modern?
universities			expensive? / students?

A: I'm sure…has more people than… **B:** That's right. But I think…is more exciting than…

5 Keep talking!

Student A go to page 132 and Student B go to page 134 for more practice.

I can compare human-made structures. ✓

B I don't believe it!

1 Interactions   Interesting and unknown facts

A What are the oldest human-made structures in your country? How old are they?

B 🎧 Listen to the conversation. What question can't Rachel answer? Then practice the conversation.

Rachel   This is pretty interesting. Look at this.

Keith   What's that?

Rachel   I'm looking at this website about the statues on Easter Island. It says they've found almost 900 statues.

Keith   No way!

Rachel   Yes. Most of the statues face inland. Only a few of them face the sea.

Keith   When did the Easter Islanders make them?

Rachel   Let's see. . . . About 500 to 750 years ago.

Keith   They look so heavy, don't they?

Rachel   Yes, they do.

Keith   How did they move them?

Rachel   I really don't know. But let's see if we can find out.

C 🎧 Read the expressions below. Complete each box with a similar expression from the conversation. Then listen and check your answers.

Expressing disbelief	Saying you don't know
_____	_____
(Seriously?)	(I have no idea.)
(I don't believe it!)	(I don't have a clue.)

D **PAIR WORK** Continue the conversation in Part B with these questions and answers. Use the expressions in Part C.

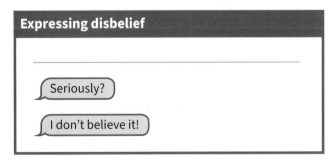

How tall is the tallest statue?	more than 20 meters tall!
Why did they stop building them?	(say you don't know)
How far is Easter Island from Chile?	more than 3,200 kilometers!
Do you think you'll ever go there?	(say you don't know)

2 **Pronunciation** Intonation in tag questions

A 🎧 **Listen and repeat. Notice the falling intonation in tag questions when the speaker expects the listener to agree or expects something to be true.**

The statues look so heavy, don't they?   The island is beautiful, isn't it?

B PAIR WORK **Practice the tag questions. Pay attention to your intonation.**

1 Easter Island is part of Chile, isn't it?

2 You read that online, didn't you?

3 She wasn't sure, was she?

4 You've never been there, have you?

5 We should go there, shouldn't we?

6 They'll probably go there, won't they?

3 **Listening** "Manhattan of the Desert"

A 🎧 **Listen to two people talk about the city of Shibam, in Yemen. Number the questions from 1 to 5 in the order you hear them.**

☐ Is it easy to get to? _____

☐ How many people live there? _____

☐ What's it famous for? _____

☐ How high are the tallest buildings? _____

☐ How old is the city? _____

B 🎧 **Listen again. Answer the questions in Part A.**

4 **Speaking** Did you know . . .?

A **Make a list of three interesting facts about human-made structures.**

> 1. There used to be soccer games and bullfights in Plaza Mayor in Madrid, Spain.
>
> 2. More people ride the Tokyo Metro in Japan each year than any other subway system in the world.
>
> 3. The TV screen in the AT&T Stadium in Dallas, Texas, is almost 50 meters long!

B GROUP WORK **Share your interesting facts. Your group expresses disbelief and asks questions for more information. If you don't know the answers to their questions, say you don't know.**

A: Did you know that there used to be soccer games and bullfights in Plaza Mayor in Madrid, Spain?

B: Bullfights? Seriously? Why is it famous?

A: I don't have a clue.

C **How many questions could you answer correctly about the structures on your list? Which classmate could answer the most questions?**

I can express disbelief. ✓

I can say that I don't know something. ✓

47

World geography

1 Vocabulary Geographical features

A 🎧 **Match the descriptions and the pictures. Then listen and check your answers.**

a The largest **desert** in Asia is the Gobi Desert.

b There are about 17,000 **islands** in Indonesia.

c Siberia's Lake Baikal is the world's deepest **lake**.

d The Indian **Ocean** covers 20% of the earth's surface.

e **Rain forests** cover almost 75% of Brunei.

f China's Yangtze River is the longest **river** in Asia.

g Langtang Valley is one of the prettiest **valleys** in Nepal.

h The highest **waterfall** in India is Jog Falls.

 1

 2

 3

 4

 5

 6

 7

 8

B **PAIR WORK** **What's another example of each geographical feature? Tell your partner.**

2 Conversation Welcome to Bali.

A 🎧 **Listen to the conversation. When does Bali get a lot of rain?**

Guide Welcome to Bali, one of the most beautiful islands in the world.

Sam It's definitely the most beautiful island I've ever visited. Is Bali the biggest island in Indonesia?

Guide No. Actually, it's one of the smallest, but it has a lot of people. The island of Java has the most people.

Sam Is that right? The weather seems pretty nice right now. Is this the best time of year to visit?

Guide Oh, yes. It's the dry season. We get the most sunshine this time of year. The wettest time is from November to April.

Sam Well, that's good. Um, what's that?

Guide Oh. It looks like rain.

B 🎧 **Listen to the rest of the conversation. Why is Sam visiting Bali?**

3 Grammar 🎧 Superlatives with adjectives and nouns

> *Use the* -est *ending or* the most *to express the superlative with adjectives.*
>
> **The wettest** time is from November to April.
> Bali is **the most beautiful** island I've ever visited.
> The dry season is **the best** time to visit.
>
> *Use* the most *to express the superlative with nouns.*
>
> Java has **the most people** of all the islands in Indonesia.
> Bali gets **the most sunshine** in the dry season.

A Complete the conversations with the superlative forms of the adjectives. Then practice with a partner.

A   I'm thinking of visiting Chile next year.

B   Great! You should try to visit my hometown, Viña del Mar.
One of _____ (popular) beaches in the country is there. It's north of Santiago.

A   OK. Should I try to go to the Atacama Desert?

B   Definitely. I think it's _____ (beautiful) part of the country.
It's one of _____ (dry) places in the world, too.

A   Cool. And how about Patagonia?

B   Well, that's in the south. Remember, Chile is _____ (long) country in the world. It takes time to see it all.

A   When's _____ (good) time to visit?

B   Anytime is fine. But I think _____ (nice) time is between November and May.

The Atacama Desert, Chile

B **PAIR WORK**   Make true sentences about your country with the phrases below.

the most cars	the most fun	the most rain	the most tourists

4 Speaking Tell me about it.

A **GROUP WORK**   Discuss your experiences in different geographical locations.

- What's the most beautiful island you've ever seen?
- What's the coldest lake, river, or ocean you've ever swum in?
- What's the highest mountain you've ever climbed?
- What's the prettiest geographical location you've ever taken a picture of?
- What's the most amazing place you've ever walked through?

B Share your information. Who has had the most interesting experience?

5 Keep talking!

Go to page 133 for more practice.

I can ask and talk about geographical features.   ✓

D Natural wonders

1 Reading 🎧

A What do you think is the most amazing natural wonder in the world? Why?

B Read the article. What are the seven wonders, and where are they?

SEVEN WONDERS OF THE NATURAL WORLD

Here is a list of some of the most fascinating places in the world.

Located in the Himalayas on the border of Nepal and Tibet, Mount Everest is the highest mountain in the world – and one of the most dangerous to climb. But that doesn't stop people from trying to get to the top of it every year!

Over five million people visit the Grand Canyon in the U.S. state of Arizona every year. The breathtaking landscape is 445 kilometers long, 24 kilometers wide, and more than a kilometer deep!

Paricutín Volcano in Mexico is more than 300 meters high, but it used to be a flat cornfield. In 1943, people saw the earth steam and crack. It grew into a new volcano in just two years!

The Rio de Janeiro Harbor in Brazil is one of the biggest and most amazing harbors in the world. It has beautiful beaches and the famous Sugar Loaf Mountain.

Have you ever heard the crashing sound of millions of liters of water? The Zambezi River between Zambia and Zimbabwe falls 120 meters, making Victoria Falls one of the largest and loudest waterfalls on the planet.

The Great Barrier Reef is not just one colorful coral reef. It's actually almost 3,000 of them! Many plants and gorgeous tropical fish live among these reefs off the coast of Australia.

The Northern Lights are exactly what their name suggests: bright, flashing lights of amazing shapes and colors in the northern sky. The North Pole has the best view of them.

C Read the article again. Complete the sentences with the correct natural wonders.

1 _____ has beautiful beaches.

2 _____ is a very loud waterfall.

3 _____ is over a kilometer deep.

4 _____ formed in two years.

5 _____ change in shape and color.

6 _____ is off a country's coast.

D **PAIR WORK** Rank the natural wonders from 1 (most amazing) to 7 (least amazing). Then compare answers.

2 Listening The Great Barrier Reef

A 🎧 **Listen to a guide talk to two tourists at the Great Barrier Reef. Which statements surprise the tourists? Check (✓) the correct answers.**

☐ The Great Barrier Reef is made up of many smaller reefs.

☐ You can see the reef from space.

☐ You can see turtles near the reef.

☐ Global warming can make the coral appear white.

B 🎧 **Listen again. Answer the questions.**

1 How many kinds of coral are there? _____

2 How does the coral look on TV? _____

3 What's the weather like today? _____

4 What does the guide say to do? _____

3 Writing A natural wonder

A Think of a natural wonder in your country.

● Where is it? _____

● What does it look like? _____

● What can you do there? _____

● When's a good time to go there? _____

B Write a paragraph about the natural wonder. Use the model and your answers in Part A to help you.

A Wonderful Mountain

Mount Toubkal is the highest mountain in Morocco, and one of the prettiest. The most popular time to visit is the summer. Many people climb the mountain, and you can hike it in two days. To me, the most interesting time to visit is the winter because you can ski. This is surprising to many people. . . .

C GROUP WORK Share your paragraphs. Can anyone add more information?

4 Speaking Seven wonders of my country

A PAIR WORK Make a list of the top seven natural or human-made wonders in your country. Why are they wonderful? Take notes.

B CLASS ACTIVITY Share your lists and reasons. Then vote on the top seven wonders to create one list.

I can describe natural wonders in my country. ✓

Wrap-up

1 Quick pair review

Lesson A `Brainstorm!`

Make a list of human-made wonders. How many do you know? You have one minute.

Lesson B `Do you remember?`

Is the sentence expressing disbelief, or is it saying you don't know? Write D (disbelief) or DK (don't know). You have one minute.

1 I have no idea. _____
2 Seriously? _____
3 No way! _____

4 I don't believe it! _____
5 I don't have a clue. _____
6 I really don't know. _____

Lesson C `Test your partner!`

Say three comparative adjectives. Can your partner use the superlative forms in a sentence? Take turns. You have three minutes.

A: More famous.

B: The most famous. The most famous person I've ever met is George Clooney.

Lesson D `Guess!`

Describe a natural wonder in your country, but don't say its name. Can your partner guess what it is? You have two minutes.

2 In the real world

What are the seven wonders of the modern world? Go online or to a library, and find information in English about the seven wonders of the modern world. Choose one and write about it.

A Wonder of the Modern World

The Itaipu Dam is one of the seven wonders of the modern world. It's on the Paraná River between Brazil and Paraguay. Many people in South America depend on the dam for power and electricity. About 40,000 workers helped construct the dam, and it's one of the most expensive objects ever built. It's also huge. In fact, it's so big that . . .

6 Organizing your time

Lesson A
- Commitments
- Present tenses used for future

Lesson B
- Offering to take a message
- Leaving a message

Lesson C
- Favors
- Requests; promises and offers with *will*

Lesson D
- Reading "Time and Culture"
- Writing: Tips for success

Warm Up

A Look at the pictures. What's happening? Do you think the people in the photos organize their time well?

B Do you think you organize your time well? Why or why not?

A | A busy week

1 ## Vocabulary Commitments

A 🎧 Match the words in columns A and B. Then listen and check your answers.

	A	B
1	a birthday	appointment
2	a blind	call
3	a business	date
4	a conference	interview
5	a doctor's	lesson
6	a job	meeting
7	soccer	party
8	a violin	practice

B **PAIR WORK** When was the last time you had each commitment? Tell your partner.

2 ## Language in context Weekend plans

A 🎧 Read George's plans for the weekend. Number the pictures from 1 to 8.

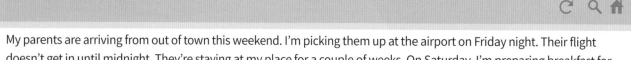

My parents are arriving from out of town this weekend. I'm picking them up at the airport on Friday night. Their flight doesn't get in until midnight. They're staying at my place for a couple of weeks. On Saturday, I'm preparing breakfast for them. Then I have a doctor's appointment. In the afternoon, I'm taking them for a drive around town. In the evening, I'm starting a new part-time job. There's a new movie I want to see on Sunday. I'm going with a friend of mine from school. It starts at 9:00 p.m., so we're having dinner first.

B Which things in Part A do you think George will enjoy? Do you have any of the same plans?

3 Grammar ∩ Present tenses used for future

> Use the present continuous to describe plans or intentions.
>
> My parents **are arriving** from out of town this weekend.
> They**'re staying** at my place for the weekend.
>
> *Use the simple present to describe events that are on a schedule or a timetable.*
>
> I **have** an appointment in the morning.
> The movie **starts** at 9:00 p.m.

A Complete the conversation with the present continuous or the simple present forms of the verbs. Then practice with a partner.

A What _____ you _____ (do) tonight?

B Oh, I _____ (take) my sister to the airport. She _____ (go) to Manila.

Her flight _____ (leave) at 9:00.

A _____ you _____ (do) anything tomorrow?

B I _____ (have) soccer practice at 2:00.

B PAIR WORK What are your plans after class? Tell your partner.

4 Listening A weekend away

A ∩ Listen to Peter talk with his neighbor Nancy. Check (✓) the true sentences.

1 ☐ Nancy has a date this weekend. _____

2 ☐ Peter's train leaves Friday night at 8:30. _____

3 ☐ Peter's grandfather is turning 70. _____

4 ☐ Peter and Kevin are going to museums on Sunday. _____

5 ☐ Peter and Kevin arrive home on Sunday evening. _____

6 ☐ Peter has a job interview on Monday. _____

B ∩ Listen again. Correct the false sentences.

5 Speaking What are you doing this weekend?

A CLASS ACTIVITY Find classmates who are going to do each thing. Write their names and ask questions for more information.

Find someone who . . . this weekend.	Name	Extra information
is going out		
is planning to stay home		
has a lesson or an appointment		
plans to meet friends		
is spending time with relatives		

B Who has the most interesting plans? What are they?

6 Keep talking!

Go to page 135 for more practice.

I can ask and talk about weekend plans. ✓

55

B Can I take a message?

Interactions Phone messages

A How many phone calls do you make in a week? Do you leave many messages?

B 🎧 Listen to the conversation. What message does Rex leave for Jake?
Then practice the conversation.

Ben	Hello?
Rex	Hi. Can I please speak to Jake?
Ben	Um, sorry. Jake's not here right now. I think he might be at the gym. Can I take a message?
Rex	Uh, sure. This is Rex Hanson. I'm calling about our class trip. Please tell him that we're leaving tomorrow at 8:00, not 9:00.
Ben	OK, got it. I'll give him the message.
Rex	Great. Thanks a lot. Bye.
Ben	Good-bye.

C 🎧 Read the expressions below. Complete each box with a similar expression from
the conversation. Then listen and check your answers.

Offering to take a message	Leaving a message
_____	_____
Do you want to leave a message?	Can you tell . . . that . . . ?
Would you like to leave a message?	Could you let . . . know that . . . ?

D PAIR WORK Have conversations like the one in Part B. Use these ideas.

You're calling your friend Carrie at home, but she's at soccer practice. She needs to bring her laptop to class.	You're calling your friend Gary at work, but he's in a meeting. The birthday party starts at 7:00, not 8:00.

2 Listening Taking messages

A 🎧 Listen to four people leave phone messages. Number the messages from 1 to 4.

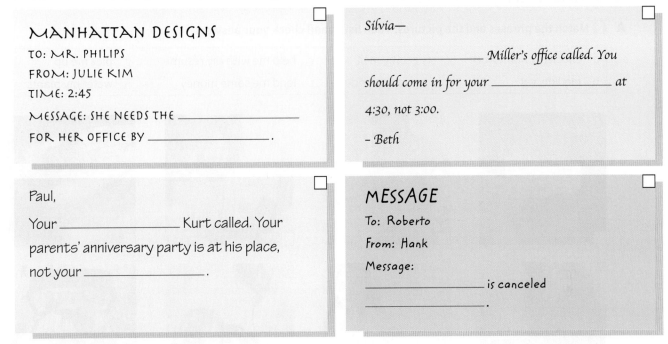

MANHATTAN DESIGNS

TO: MR. PHILIPS

FROM: JULIE KIM

TIME: 2:45

MESSAGE: SHE NEEDS THE _____

FOR HER OFFICE BY _____ .

Silvia—

_____ Miller's office called. You

should come in for your _____ at

4:30, not 3:00.

- Beth

Paul,

Your _____ Kurt called. Your

parents' anniversary party is at his place,

not your _____ .

MESSAGE

To: Roberto

From: Hank

Message:

_____ is canceled

_____ .

B 🎧 Listen again. Complete the messages.

C 🎧 Listen to the people return the calls. What happens to whom? Write M (Mr. Philips),
P (Paul), R (Roberto), or S (Silvia).

1 _____ gets a busy signal. 3 _____ leaves a voicemail.

2 _____ gets disconnected. 4 _____ calls the wrong number.

3 Speaking Role play

A Complete the chart with your own ideas.

	Who's the message for?	What's the message about?	What's the message?
1	Rosario	soccer practice	She needs to come 15 minutes early.
2		the meeting	It's on Thursday, not Tuesday. It's still at 4:00.
3	Jennifer		It starts at 10:00p.m. Bring dancing shoes.
4		the job interview	
5			

B PAIR WORK Role-play the phone conversations. Then change roles.

Student A: Call the people in the chart. They can't talk, so leave messages for them.

Student B: Answer the phone. Explain why the people can't talk, and offer to take
messages for them.

I can offer to take a message. ☑

I can leave a message. ☑

C Can you do me a favor?

1 Vocabulary Favors

A 🎧 Match the phrases and the pictures. Then listen and check your answers.

a check my homework	c get my mail	e help me with my résumé	g pick me up
b feed my cat	d give me a ride	f lend me some money	h water my plants

 1 ☐

 2 ☐

 3 ☐

 4 ☐

 5 ☐

 6 ☐

 7 ☐

 8 ☐

B **PAIR WORK** Who might you ask to do each thing in Part A? Discuss your ideas.

| a child | a classmate | a friend | a neighbor | a parent | a teacher |

2 Conversation Is that all?

A 🎧 Listen to the conversation. What things does Kate ask Ruth to do for her?

Ruth   Oh, hi, Kate. What's up?

Kate   Hi, Ruth. Listen, I'm going away this weekend. Can you do me a favor?

Ruth   Sure. What do you need?

Kate   Can you feed my cat, please?

Ruth   No problem. I'll feed her. Is that all?

Kate   Well, could you please get my mail, too?

Ruth   Sure. I could do that for you. I'll put it on your kitchen table. Anything else?

Kate   If you don't mind, there's one more thing.

Ruth   What's that?

Kate   I'm getting back at 11:00 on Sunday night. Would you mind picking me up at the airport?

B 🎧 Listen to the rest of the conversation. Why can't Ruth pick Kate up?

3 Grammar 🎧 Requests; promises and offers with *will*

Requests	Promises and offers
Can you **feed** my cat, please?	No problem. **I'll feed** her.
Could you please **get** my mail?	Sure. **I'll put** it on your kitchen table.
Would you **pick** me up at the airport?	All right. **I won't be** late. I promise.
Would you **mind picking** me up at the airport?	No, I don't mind. **I'll be** there.

A Match the requests and the responses. Then practice with a partner.

1 Can you lend me your car tonight? _____

2 Ms. Smith, would you check my homework, please? _____

3 Can you give me a ride to class? _____

4 Would you mind feeding my fish? _____

5 Could you water my plants this weekend? _____

6 Would you mind picking me up at the mall? _____

a. Sure. I'll look at it after I help Michael.

b. No problem. I'll do it on Saturday.

c. Not at all. What time?

d. I guess so. I'll give you the keys after I pick up Rachel from school.

e. Yeah, sure. I'll be at your house at 10:00.

f. No, I don't mind. I'll feed them after work.

B **PAIR WORK** Ask and answer the questions in Part A. Answer with your own offer or promise.

4 Pronunciation Reduction of *could you* and *would you*

A 🎧 Listen and repeat. Notice how *could you* and *would you* are sometimes pronounced /kʊdʒə/ and /wʊdʒə/.

Could you please get my mail?   **Would you** pick me up at the airport?

B **PAIR WORK** Practice requests with *could you*, *would you*, and the phrases from Exercise 1. Reduce *could you* and *would you*.

5 Speaking Unfavorable favors

A Think of three favors to ask your classmates. Use the ideas below or your own ideas. Be creative!

feed my pet snake	lend me some money
check my homework	lend me your cell phone
help me clean my room	make my lunch

B **CLASS ACTIVITY** Find three different classmates to do the favors for you. If you decline a request, make an excuse. If you accept a request, make an offer or a promise.

6 Keep talking!

Go to page 136 for more practice.

I can make requests, promises, and offers. ✓

D Perspectives on time

1 Reading 🎧

A Do you have a busy schedule? Or do you find time to relax?

B Read the article. Do you identify more with the Germans or Italians?

PERSPECTIVE ON TIME

Time and Culture

Imagine you're going to a party this weekend at your friend's apartment. "Could you come at 7 p.m. and bring dessert?" she asked. What time do you think you'll actually arrive? Ten minutes early? Half an hour late? Right on time?

The answer probably depends on your cultural view of time. Different cultures and countries have very different ways of thinking about time. Even countries that are quite close to each other like Germany and Italy see time very differently.

Deadlines and Meeting Times

There is a saying in countries like Germany and the U.S., "Time is money." People think of wasting time as the same as wasting or losing money. If you miss a deadline or are late to a meeting, people might get mad. In other countries like Italy and Greece, people are less strict about deadlines and appointments. Meetings and conversations start and end when it feels right, not when the clock strikes 2 p.m.

Getting Things Done vs. Building Relationships

In many Western countries, people want to get as much done in as little time as possible. They get impatient if decisions are not made fast enough. In other countries, taking time to build relationships is more important than getting things done fast. That's why meetings often start with lots of small talk before getting down to business.

Pace of Life

In some countries, it almost seems that people are in a race to get through life as quickly and efficiently as possible. In other countries, life is more about enjoying time—sharing meals, taking walks and spending time with friends and family.

As you travel or make friends with people from other cultures, it can help to improve communication if you understand their perspectives on time.

C Read the article again. Write three differences between the way people view time in Germany and Italy.

In Germany...	In Italy...
People want to get a lot done.	People want to enjoy life.

D PAIR WORK How do you view time in your culture? What about in your family? Does everyone in one country or culture share the same view of time?

2 Writing Tips for success

A `GROUP WORK` **Choose one of the topics below or your own idea. What tips for success can you think of? Discuss your ideas and make a list of your tips.**

how to find more time for family	how to remember important things
how to make and keep friends	how to study better

B `GROUP WORK` **Create a poster with the most useful tips. Write a short paragraph for each tip.**

C `CLASS ACTIVITY` **Present your tips for success. Ask and answer questions for more information.**

3 Speaking Time management interview

> **HOW TO DEVELOP BETTER STUDY HABITS**
>
> 1 **Take regular breaks.**
>
>   It's important to take breaks. Get up and stretch, go for a walk, or call a friend for a chat. You'll feel ready for more!
>
> 2 **Listen to music.**
>
>   Listen to relaxing music. This helps you…

A `PAIR WORK` **Interview your partner. Check (✓) his or her answers.**

Are you overdoing things?

Do you…?	Often	Sometimes	Never
get nervous when you have to wait	☐	☐	☐
feel like you do things too quickly	☐	☐	☐
often do two or more things at once	☐	☐	☐
feel bad when you're not working or studying	☐	☐	☐
feel like things don't move fast enough for you	☐	☐	☐
forget important events, like birthdays	☐	☐	☐
get angry in situations you can't control	☐	☐	☐
get bored easily when you're not working or studying	☐	☐	☐
get angry when you make small mistakes	☐	☐	☐
make big decisions before you get all the facts	☐	☐	☐

B `PAIR WORK` **Score your partner's answers. Add 2 for *often*, 1 for *sometimes*, and 0 for *never*. Tell your partner the results.**

13-20 You're overdoing it.	**7-12** You're overdoing it a little.	**0-6** You're not overdoing it.
You probably already know you're too busy. Take a deep breath and slow down.	You're doing well, but try not to do too much. Make sure you make time for yourself.	Congratulations! You are managing your time well. Keep it up!

C `PAIR WORK` **Are you overdoing it? If so, what time-management tips can help? Discuss your ideas.**

Wrap-up

1 Quick pair review

Lesson A `Find out!`

What are two commitments both you and your partner have next month?
You have two minutes.

A: I'm going to a conference for work next month. Are you?

B: No, I'm not, but I have a dentist's appointment next month. Do you?

A: . . .

Lesson B `Brainstorm!`

Make a list of three ways to offer to take a message and three ways to leave one.
You have two minutes.

Lesson C `Do you remember?`

Match the requests and the responses. You have two minutes.

1 Could you water my plants for me? _____

2 Would you mind giving me a ride to work? _____

3 Can you feed my dog, please? _____

4 Could you please call me back at 4:00? _____

5 Can you meet me in the library tomorrow? _____

a. OK. I'll call your cell phone.

b. Sure. I'll water them.

c. Yes. I'll bring my books so we can study.

d. Yeah, I'll do that. What does he eat?

e. No problem. I'll pick you up at 8:00.

Lesson D `Give your opinion!`

What three tips can you give someone who is always late for class? Decide together.
You have two minutes.

2 In the real world

What are some tips for success? Go online and find tips in English about one of these
topics or your own idea. Then write about them.

how to get rich	how to make a good first impression
how to improve your pronunciation	how to write a good résumé

How to Save Money

It's important to save money every month. One way to save money is to turn off the lights when you aren't using them, because electricity is expensive. Another way to save money is to cook at home more often. Food can be very expensive, especially if you eat out a lot. You should look for discounts online. Also, . . .

Finding out more

A Read the chart. Then add two more.

Find someone who . . .	Name	Extra information
is saving money for something special		
is in a good mood today		
has one brother and one sister		
is reading an interesting book		
wants to get a pet		
is taking a different class		
works on weekends		
thinks English is fun		
hates to talk on the phone		

B **CLASS ACTIVITY** Find classmates who do or are doing each thing in Part A. Write their names. Ask questions for more information.

A: Are you saving money for something special?

B: Yes, I am.

A: Oh, really? What do you want to buy?

C **CLASS ACTIVITY** Share the most interesting information.

Similar behaviors

A Write your answers to the questions in the chart.

Questions	Me	Name: _____
1 What do you do when you can't sleep at night?		
2 What do you do if you forget to do your homework?		
3 When you feel really happy about something, what do you do?		
4 What do you do if someone tells you something that isn't true?		
5 If a friend calls you and you don't want to talk, what do you do?		
6 What do you do when you are extremely angry at someone?		

B **PAIR WORK** Interview your partner. Complete the chart with his or her answers.

A: What do you do when you can't sleep at night?

B: I usually read a book. How about you?

A: When I can't sleep at night, I always listen to music.

C **PAIR WORK** Compare your information. Do any of your partner's answers surprise you? Do you and your partner have any similar behaviors?

Keep talking!

What was happening?

A Look at this picture for two minutes. What was happening when it started to rain? Try to remember as many details as you can.

B PAIR WORK Cover the picture. Ask the questions and answer with the information you remember.

1 Where was the couple sitting when the rain started? What were they doing?
2 What was the police officer holding? What was she wearing?
3 What was the name of the café? What was on the café table?
4 What was the waiter holding? Where was he standing?
5 What was the young boy holding? What was he watching on TV?
6 What was the taxi driver doing? What was the name of the cab company?

C PAIR WORK Check your answers. How many answers did you remember correctly?

How does it end?

A PAIR WORK Imagine you are the people in one of the sets of pictures below. Tell a story that explains what happened. Choose your own ending to the story.

Story 1

Story 2

B GROUP WORK Tell your story to another pair. Can they think of another ending to your story? Which ending do you like better?

"This really happened to us. We were driving down the road in our car. The weather was very nice, and we were enjoying the ride. We were going to our friend's house. We had a map, but suddenly . . ."

C CLASS ACTIVITY Share your stories. Vote on the best one.

Keep talking!

Then and now

Student A

A **PAIR WORK** You and your partner have pictures of Chuck. You have an old picture of what he used to look like, and your partner has a new picture of what he looks like now. Describe Chuck to find the differences between then and now.

Chuck – then

A: Chuck used to have long black hair.

B: He doesn't have long hair now.

A: So that's different. He used to . . .

B **PAIR WORK** You and your partner have pictures of Amy. You have a new picture of what she looks like now, and your partner has an old picture of what she used to look like. Describe Amy to find the differences between then and now.

Amy – now

Then and now

Student B

A **PAIR WORK** You and your partner have a picture of Chuck. You have a new picture of what he looks like now, and your partner has an old picture of what he used to look like. Describe Chuck to find the differences between then and now.

Chuck – now

A: Chuck used to have long black hair.

B: He doesn't have long hair now.

A: So that's different. He used to . . .

B **PAIR WORK** You and your partner have pictures of Amy. You have an old picture of what she used to look like, and your partner has a new picture of what she looks like now. Describe Amy to find the differences between then and now.

Amy – then

Keep talking!

What's hot?

A `PAIR WORK` **Write your own example of each thing in the chart.**

Give an example of . . .	Me	Name: _____
something which looks tacky on young people		
an area of town that's extremely trendy		
a store that's very popular with young people		
a male celebrity who's really fashionable		
a female celebrity who's very glamorous		
a fashion trend that was very weird		
a fashion that you really like		
someone that has influenced fashion		

B `PAIR WORK` **Interview your partner. Complete the chart with his or her answers.**

A: What is something which you think looks tacky on young people?

B: Well, I don't like those big sunglasses that some young girls wear.
I think they're tacky.

C `CLASS ACTIVITY` **Compare your information. Do you agree with everyone's opinion? Why or why not?**

A: I think . . . is a celebrity who's very glamorous.

B: Really? I think her clothes are kind of weird.

C: I like most of the clothes that she wears. I think she has a lot of style.

Keep talking! 129

I've never . . .

A Write examples of things you've never done.

a sport I've never played:

_____

a TV show I've never watched:

_____

a food I've never eaten:

_____

a famous movie I've never seen:

_____

a restaurant I've never been to:

_____

a place I've never visited:

_____

B GROUP WORK Tell your group about the things you've never done. Ask and answer questions for more information.

A: I've never played cricket.

B: Yeah, that's not popular here at all.

C: I've never played basketball.

D: You're kidding! Never? Not even in school?

C CLASS ACTIVITY Share your information. Which answers surprised you the most?

Keep talking!

No kidding!

A Add two more questions about experiences to the chart.

Have you ever . . . ?	Me	Name: _____
seen a solar eclipse		
watched three movies in one day		
gone swimming in the rain		
gotten a postcard from overseas		
cooked a vegetarian dinner		
seen a shooting star		
had a really bad haircut		
forgotten to pay an important bill		
eaten in a French restaurant		
lost something very special to you		

a solar eclipse

a shooting star

B **PAIR WORK** Interview your partner. Complete the chart with his or her answers.

A: Have you ever seen an eclipse?

B: Yes, I have. I saw a solar eclipse once.

A: No kidding! When did you see it?

C Share the most interesting information.

Keep talking!

Impressive places

Student A

A You and your partner have information about impressive places. Do you know the answers to the questions on the left? Circle your guesses.

1 Which is taller?

   a. Eiffel Tower
      (Paris, France)

   b. CN Tower
      (Toronto, Canada)

a. ☐ 300.5 meters tall   b. ☐ _____ meters tall

2 Which is longer?

   a. Golden Gate Bridge
      (San Francisco, the U.S.A.)

   b. Harbor Bridge
      (Sydney, Australia)

a. ☐ _____ meters long   b. ☐ 1,149 meters long

3 Which is bigger?

   a. Red Square
      (Moscow, Russia)

   b. Tiananmen Square
      (Beijing, China)

a. ☐ 23,100 square meters   b. ☐ _____ square meters

4 Which has more riders?

   a. São Paulo subway system
      (Brazil)

   b. London subway system
      (the U.K.)

a. ☐ _____ riders a day   b. ☐ 4,250,000 riders a day

B **PAIR WORK** Ask and answer questions to fill in the missing information. Then check (✓) the correct answers in Part A.

	Saying large numbers	
How tall is . . . ?	**100.2**	"one hundred point two"
How long is . . . ?	**3,456**	"three thousand four hundred (and) fifty-six"
How big is . . . ?	**78,900**	"seventy-eight thousand nine hundred"
How many riders does . . . have?	**120,000**	"one hundred (and) twenty thousand"
	3,450,000	"three million four hundred (and) fifty thousand"

C **CLASS ACTIVITY** How many of your guesses were correct? Can you make more comparisons?

Keep talking!

Planning a visit

A **PAIR WORK** Imagine that a friend from another country is planning to visit you and asks you the questions in the email below. Discuss your responses.

● ● ●	Reply Forward

To: Beth <bettybeth@email.com>
From: Jane <jgal@email.com>
Date: March 17
Subject: Re: Planning my trip . . .

Hey!
Before I visit, I have some questions for you:

– What's the best way to travel around? Is it the fastest? Is it the cheapest?
– Which part of town has the best nightlife? When is the best time to go out?
– What's the most popular place for a tourist to visit? Have you been there?
– What's the most interesting traditional food to try? Where should I try it?
– What would make a nice day trip? Is it easy to get to?
– What's the best museum? What's it like? Should I go there?
– Which time of year has the nicest weather? Which has the worst?

I'm sorry that I'm asking so many questions. I'm just very excited, and I want to plan as much as I can!

Thanks in advance for the information. See you soon!

Take care,
Jane

A: The best way to travel around is by subway.

B: I think it's better to go by bus. It's faster than the subway.

B **GROUP WORK** Share your ideas with another pair. Do you have similar answers?

Keep talking!

Impressive places

Student B

A You and your partner have information about impressive places. Do you know the answers to the questions on the left? Circle your guesses.

1 Which is taller?

a. Eiffel Tower
(Paris, France)

b. CN Tower
(Toronto, Canada)

a. ☐ _____ meters tall   b. ☐ 553.3 meters tall

2 Which is longer?

a. Golden Gate Bridge
(San Francisco, the U.S.A.)

b. Harbor Bridge
(Sydney, Australia)

a. ☐ 2,737 meters long   b. ☐ _____ meters long

3 Which is bigger?

a. Red Square
(Moscow, Russia)

b. Tiananmen Square
(Beijing, China)

a. ☐ _____ square meters   b. ☐ 440,000 square meters

4 Which has more riders?

a. São Paulo subway system
(Brazil)

b. London subway system
(the U.K.)

a. ☐ 3,500,000 riders a day   b. ☐ _____ riders a day

B **PAIR WORK** Ask and answer questions to fill in the missing information. Then check (✓) the correct answers in Part A.

How tall is . . . ?

How long is . . . ?

How big is . . . ?

How many riders does . . . have?

Saying large numbers	
100.2	"one hundred point two"
3,456	"three thousand four hundred (and) fifty-six"
78,900	"seventy-eight thousand nine hundred"
120,000	"one hundred (and) twenty thousand"
3,450,000	"three million four hundred (and) fifty thousand"

C **CLASS ACTIVITY** How many of your guesses were correct? Can you make more comparisons?

Keep talking!

The next two weeks

Student A

A Complete the calendar for next week and the week after it with the correct dates and any plans you have.

Next week:

Sunday	Monday	Tuesday	Wednesday	Thursday	Friday	Saturday

The week after next:

Sunday	Monday	Tuesday	Wednesday	Thursday	Friday	Saturday

B **PAIR WORK** Ask and answer questions about your plans. Find a time to do something together.

A: What are you doing next Thursday afternoon?

B: Oh, I have my karate lesson then. What are you doing the day after that?

A: Nothing. Do you want to get together?

C **GROUP WORK** Tell another pair about the plans you made in Part B. Invite them to join you. Are they free?

A: Barry and I are getting together on Friday.

B: We're meeting at Mr. Freeze for some ice cream. Do you want to join us?

C: I'm sorry, but I can't. I have a job interview on Friday

D: I'm not free, either. I have to go grocery shopping.

A helping hand

A PAIR WORK Imagine you're the people in the pictures. Role-play the situations.

Student A: Ask Student B for a favor.

Student B: Agree to Student A's request. Offer to help, and continue the conversation.

A: Could you do me a favor? Could you please take my picture?

B: No problem. I'll take it for you.

B PAIR WORK Change roles. Role-play the new situations.

C PAIR WORK Ask each other for two more favors.

Keep talking!

Irregular verbs

Base form	Simple past	Past participle
be	was, were	been
become	became	become
break	broke	broken
build	built	built
buy	bought	bought
choose	chose	chosen
come	came	come
do	did	done
draw	drew	drawn
drink	drank	drunk
drive	drove	driven
eat	ate	eaten
fall	fell	fallen
feel	felt	felt
fly	flew	flown
forget	forgot	forgotten
get	got	gotten
give	gave	given
go	went	gone
hang	hung	hung
have	had	had
hear	heard	heard
hold	held	held
know	knew	known
leave	left	left

Base form	Simple past	Past participle
lose	lost	lost
make	made	made
meet	met	met
pay	paid	paid
put	put	put
read	read	read
ride	rode	ridden
run	ran	run
say	said	said
see	saw	seen
sell	sold	sold
send	sent	sent
sing	sang	sung
sit	sat	sat
sleep	slept	slept
speak	spoke	spoken
spend	spent	spent
stand	stood	stood
swim	swam	swum
take	took	taken
teach	taught	taught
think	thought	thought
wear	wore	worn
win	won	won
write	wrote	written

Adjective and adverb formations

Adjectives	Adverbs	Adjectives	Adverbs
agreeable	agreeably	immature	immaturely
amazing	amazingly	impatient	impatiently
ambitious	ambitiously	inconsiderate	inconsiderately
angry	angrily	indecisive	indecisively
brave	bravely	interesting	interestingly
careful	carefully	late	late
confident	confidently	lucky	luckily
considerate	considerately	mature	maturely
creative	creatively	nervous	nervously
curious	curiously	optimistic	optimistically
decisive	decisively	patient	patiently
disagreeable	disagreeably	quick	quickly
dishonest	dishonestly	rare	rarely
early	early	reliable	reliably
easy	easily	sad	sadly
enthusiastic	enthusiastically	serious	seriously
extreme	extremely	similar	similarly
fair	fairly	strange	strangely
fashionable	fashionably	stubborn	stubbornly
fast	fast	sudden	suddenly
fortunate	fortunately	surprising	surprisingly
glamorous	glamorously	unfair	unfairly
good	well	unfortunate	unfortunately
hard	hard	unreliable	unreliably
honest	honestly	wise	wisely

Credits

The authors and publishers acknowledge the following sources of copyright material and are grateful for the permissions granted. While every effort has been made, it has not always been possible to identify the sources of all the material used, or to trace all copyright holders. If any omissions are brought to our notice, we will be happy to include the appropriate acknowledgements on reprinting and in the next update to the digital edition, as applicable.

Photography

All the photographs are sourced from Getty Images.

U1: Steve Debenport/E+; Hero Images; PeopleImages/DigitalVision; sturti/E+; Kwanchai Lerttanapunyaporn/EyeEm; ArisSu/iStock/Getty Images Plus; bonniej/E+; Tim Hall/Cultura; Lee Pettet/Stockbyte; Ca-ssis/iStock/Getty Images Plus; kali9/E+; studo58/iStock/Getty Images Plus; Peter Zvonar/Moment Open; paylessimages/iStock/Getty Images Plus; Caiaimage/Sam Edwards; James Griffiths Photography/iStock/Getty Images Plus; Simon McGill/Moment; 9wut/iStock/Getty Images Plus; trekandshoot/iStock/Getty Images Plus; Design Pics/Craig Tuttle; Chris Ryan/OJO Images; Rob Lewine; Maksim Kamyshanskii/iStock/Getty Images Plus; winhorse/iStock/Getty Images Plus; JGI/Jamie Grill/Blend Images; Lívia Fernandes - Brazil./Moment; Imgorthand/E+; BONNINSTUDIO/iStock/Getty Images Plus; JGI/Jamie Grill/Tetra images; quavondo/E+; **U2:** Blend Images - KidStock/Brand X Pictures; Geber86/E+; KatarzynaBialasiewicz/iStock/Getty Images Plus; PeopleImages/E+; Eric Audras/ONOKY; Tetra Images; groveb/iStock/Getty Images Plus; KiraVolkov/iStock/Getty Images Plus; Paul Bradbury/OJO Images; tazytaz/E+; Caiaimage/Tom Merton; Peter Dazeley/Photographer's Choice; Buena Vista Images/DigitalVision; PeopleImages/DigitalVision; George Doyle/Stockbyte; Lew Robertson/Corbis; ©David J Spurdens; Fuse; Juanmonino/E+; Jupiterimages/The Image Bank; NicolasMcComber/E+; cirano83/iStock/Getty Images Plus; Peter Dazeley/Photographer's Choice; MASSIVE/Stone; Image Source/DigitalVision; Peter Dazeley/Photographer's Choice; **U3:** Hoxton/Tom Merton; Eamonn McCormack/BFC/Getty Images Entertainment; Viktorcvetkovic/E+; Lorado/E+; castillodominici/iStock/Getty Images Plus; Peter Dazeley/Photographer's Choice; Trinette Reed; Tvi Nguyen/EyeEm; Chauncey James/EyeEm; Dirk Saeger/EyeEm; CraigRJD/iStock/Getty Images Plus; Yagi Studio/DigitalVision; Nemia Walter/EyeEm; Phil Boorman/Cultura; Christophel Fine Art/UIG via Getty Images; The Art Collector/Print Collector; Brandon Colbert Photography/Moment; istanbulimage/E+; yasinguneysu/iStock/Getty Images Plus; ksevgi/iStock/Getty Images Plus; stuartbur/iStock/Getty Images Plus; nortongo/iStock/Getty Images Plus; NAKphotos/iStock/Getty Images Plus; Kay-Paris Fernandes/WireImage; Tetra Images; andresr/E+; Indeed; Mimi Haddon/DigitalVision; Morsa Images/DigitalVision; PeopleImages/E+; photosindia; fotostorm/E+; feedough/iStock/Getty Images Plus; Viktoria Ovcharenko/iStock/Getty Images Plus; FangXiaNuo/E+; Michele Quattrin/mQn Photography/Moment; soleg/iStock/Getty Images Plus; Drazen_/E+; Fabrice LEROUGE/ONOKY; **U4:** RelaxFoto.de/E+; Graiki/Moment; Alexander Jackson/EyeEm; Hill Street Studios/DigitalVision; gpointstudio/iStock/Getty Images Plus; guruXOOX/iStock/Getty Images Plus; TAGSTOCK1/iStock/Getty Images Plus; kali9/E+; Ivanko_Brnjakovic/iStock/Getty Images Plus; andresr/iStock/Getty Images Plus; Elena KHarchenko/iStock/Getty Images Plus; ONOKY - Fabrice LEROUGE/Brand X Pictures; Martin Harvey/Photolibrary; Georgijevic/E+ perfect loop/iStock/Getty Images Plus; Vitalalp/iStock/Getty Images Plus; Pierre-Yves Babelon/Moment; Carso80/iStock Editorial/Getty Images Plus; massimo colombo/Moment; Stewart Cohen/Blend Images; James Osmond/Photolibrary; kimkole/iStock/Getty Images Plus; PeopleImages/DigitalVision; LWA/Dann Tardif/Blend Images; StockFood; Colin Anderson Productions pty ltd/DigitalVision; Trinette Reed/Blend Images; Ricardo Liberato/Moment; DAVID NUNUK/Science Photo Library; Carlos Fernandez/Moment; **U5:** dblight/E+; Ibon Bastida/EyeEm; Dan77/iStock/Getty Images Plus; Guillaume CHANSON/Moment; Mark Miller Photos/DigitalVision; Christian Ender/Getty Images News; Patricia Hamilton/Moment; ChandraDhas/iStock; Tina Llorca/EyeEm; QQ7/iStock/Getty Images Plus; Pley/iStock/Getty Images Plus; David Madison/Corbis; Kadshah Nagibe/EyeEm; FrankvandenBergh/iStock/Getty Images Plus; Alexander Spatari/Moment; isitsharp/iStock; JAWOC/AFP; Fuse; Feifei Cui-Paoluzzo/Moment; Santiago Urquijo/Moment; Ivan_off/iStock/Getty Images Plus; Alexander Bennett/EyeEm; Tunach/iStock/Getty Images Plus; grebcha/iStock/Getty Images Plus; G-o-o-d-M-a-n/iStock/Getty Images Plus; Robin Smith/The Image Bank; IndiaPictures/Universal Images Group; JaySi/iStock/Getty Images Plus; Michele Falzone/The Image Bank; Feng Wei Photography/Moment; Torresigner/iStock/Getty Images Plus; DeAgostini/G. SIOEN; Daniel Osterkamp/Moment; halecr/E+; Arctic-Images/Corbis Documentary; Tammy616/iStock/Getty Images Plus; Nasser Mar/EyeEm; Antonello/Moment Open; Matteo Colombo/DigitalVision; Roberto Machado Noa/LightRocket; Justin Sullivan/Getty Images News; xavierarnau/E+; DEA/W. BUSS/De Agostin; Lintao Zhang/Getty Images Entertainment; Victor Moriyama/Getty Images News; Photography taken by Mario Gutiérrez./Moment; Medioimages/Photodisc; **U6:** denozy/iStock/Getty Images Plus; AJ_Watt/E+; Geber86/E+; Sam Edwards/OJO Images; skynesher/E+; Rob Daly/OJO Images; Terry Vine/Blend Images; Education Images/Universal Images Group; Blue Jean Images; PeopleImages/E+; LeoPatrizi/E+; Warren Photography/Warren Photography; JGI/Jamie Grill/Blend Images; kali9/iStock/Getty Images Plus; Westend61; Oleh_Slobodeniuk/E+; filadendron/E+; blackred/E+; Westend61; alikemalkarasu/E+; xxmmxx/E+; Wavebreakmedia/iStock/Getty Images Plus; Klaus Vedfelt/Riser; Erik Isakson/Blend Images; **U7:** sanjeri/E+; VCG/Contributor/Visual China Group; Kevin Dodge/Corbis; Jamie Grill; Lorado/E+; Lumina Images/Blend Images; powerofforever/E+; Tribalium/iStock; Hill Creek Pictures/UpperCut Images; Steve Debenport/E+; Cate Gillon/Staff/Getty Images News; ivanastar/iStock/Getty Images Plus; MatiasEnElMundo/iStock/Getty Images Plus; Deepak Sethi/iStock/Getty Images Plus; MangoStar_Studio/iStock/Getty Images Plus; Westend61; Jose Luis Pelaez Inc/Blend Images; **U8:** Erik Von Weber; Coldimages/iStock/Getty Images Plus; grafvision/iStock/Getty Images Plus; catalby/iStock/Getty Images Plus; Michel Tripepi/EyeEm; drnadig/E+; Krakozawr/E+; Grace Cary/Moment; baona/iStock/Getty Images Plus; Michael Burrell iStock/Getty Images Plus; kasto80/iStock/Getty Images Plus; Wavebreak Media/Getty Images